Easy Does It Dating Guide

Easy Does It Dating Guide

For People in Recovery

Mary Faulkner *

Hazelden
Center City, Minnesota 55012-0176

1-800-328-0094
1-651-213-4590 (Fax)
www.hazelden.org

Library of Congress Cataloging-in-Publication Data

Faulkner, Mary, M.A.
   Easy does it dating guide : for people in recovery / Mary
   Faulkner.
      p. cm.
   Includes bibliographical references and index.
   ISBN 1-59285-100-2 (paperback)
      1. Recovering alcoholics. 2. Recovering addicts. 3. Dating
   (Social customs) 4. Interpersonal relations. I. Title.

HV5275.F28 2004
646.7'7'0874—dc22

                                                        2004047420

08 07 06 05 04   6 5 4 3 2 1

Editor's note
The stories in this book are composites of actual situations. Any
resemblance to specific persons, living or dead, or specific events
is entirely coincidental.

Cover design by Theresa Gedig
Interior design by Rachel Holscher
Typesetting by Stanton Publication Services, Inc.

Contents

Gratitude List   vii

Introduction   ix

Chapter One   Clean-and-Sober Dating:
The Ultimate Reality Show   1

Chapter Two   Dating: A Need or "Amuck"?   17

Chapter Three   Getting Different Results   39

Chapter Four   Boundaries: We're Not Talking
County Line   53

Chapter Five   Meet the Committee   71

Chapter Six   Into Action: Where to Go and
What to Do   89

Chapter Seven   The HOW of Dating and Relating   113

Chapter Eight   Sex, Single, and Staying Sober   135

Chapter Nine   Variations on a Theme   159

Chapter Ten   Breaking Up: Damage Control   177

Epilogue   195

Appendix A: Homework for Extra Credit   197

Appendix B: Suggested Readings   209

Appendix C: The Twelve Steps of Alcoholics
Anonymous   211

Index   213

About the Author   221

Gratitude List

My deepest gratitude is to the founders of Alcoholic Anonymous for the Twelve Steps and Twelve Traditions that are the foundation of this book. Likewise, many thanks to the community of recovering people all over the world whose wit and wisdom are sprinkled throughout these pages. Over the years I have had the opportunity to hear many people's stories and be a part of their healing process. I am constantly amazed at the luminosity of the human spirit and the total adaptability of Twelve Step principles to all life's challenges.

I am grateful to pioneers Melody Beattie, John Bradshaw, Anne Wilson Schaef, Pia Mellody, Terence Gorski, Patrick Carnes, Robin Norwood, and others who have unraveled many of the mysteries around addiction—putting names on family-of-origin issues, introducing us to our inner child, and freeing us from codependency. Their work continues to teach, inform, and heal. Without their work, this book would not be possible.

I'm grateful to many people who have directly been a part of this book—my agent, Linda Roghaar, my editor, Karen Chernyaev, Theo Gund for her encouragement, and Hazelden for publishing this work.

In respect of the tradition of anonymity, and just because it would be impossible to name everyone involved, I'd like to extend my gratitude to all who have dared to step out of the mainstream and try a different way of living!

Introduction

The *Easy Does It Dating Guide* is for men and women of all ages in recovery from any and all addictive substances or behaviors. Suggestions apply to male and female dating as well as same-sex relationships (the use of *he* and *she* is alternated throughout the text and readers are encouraged to adjust pronouns appropriately). The book takes you through preparing to date, dating, selecting a partner, and moving from dating to relating—applying recovery principles to each stage of the process. When the book mentions *program, Steps,* or *Traditions,* it is specifically referring to Twelve Step recovery programs as described in the books and literature produced by Alcoholics Anonymous World Services, Inc., in New York.

The Twelve Steps and Twelve Traditions of Alcoholics Anonymous, as well as the folk wisdom that circulates throughout the recovering community, has much to teach us about the nature of relationships—whether between friends, lovers, or married partners. Hopefully the *Easy Does It Dating Guide* will begin the process of applying recovery theory to your desire to date, relate, and mate in a healthy way. As you read this book, remember that the model of healthy dating presented here is the *ideal.* We rally around the flag of progress not perfection, so read the material, talk about it with friends and sponsors, and give yourself plenty of time to learn and grow.

Chapter One ✱

Clean-and-Sober Dating:
The Ultimate Reality Show

- Would I recognize a healthy date if I saw one?
- Does addiction leave a mark on my permanent record?
- What about "sport" dating?
- Relationship hell: dating traps you can avoid.

Definition of dating: *a social or romantic engagement with another person*

Definition of dating in recovery: *a subject that makes the blood run cold*

The subject of dating is practically taboo in many recovery circles—dodged with the vigor reserved for sidestepping a cobra. If you don't believe it, just mention *relationship* during an Alcoholics Anonymous (AA) meeting and eyes roll, heads drop, and the groaning begins. What's being expressed depends on whom you ask. No doubt some in the room are recalling their last failed attempt, and others are afraid of trying; neither group wants to be reminded of the situation, wishing the whole topic would just go away. Beneath all the grumbling and foot shuffling is the fact that most folks in recovery are struggling with the whole business of relationships, including dating, intimacy, and commitment. The majority have little to draw on by way of

1

healthy examples or experiences, yet the hope for that always-elusive good relationship doesn't go away.

EAST OF EDEN

What is true for recovering people might well be true among the general population as well. One has only to look at the explosion of dating services as well as the divorce rate to see that most people haven't discovered the magic formula for successful relationships—yet we all keep trying. Ever since Adam and Eve donned fig leaves and hiked out of paradise, we've been following in their footsteps. The urge for "together-ing" can be about anything from keeping the human race going to keeping our feet warm on a cold night. Either way, you'd think by now we would have gotten better at it—but regardless, we keep hoping. Why? The desire to form an intimate and lasting tie with another human being is a reasonable expectation.

In addition to the challenges almost everyone faces in dating and relating, people recovering from addiction have a couple of particular dragons to slay, making clean-and-sober dating seem like the ultimate reality show. Dating in recovery has been compared to playing football without gear, running barefoot over sharp rocks, and having dental work without the benefit of painkillers. It can be the great escape, bounce you back into relapse, or trigger a new addiction.

So why do we it? Because we also learn to love and be loved, we gain insight about ourselves, and we grow spiritually—all through relationships. Bonding and developing intimacy are natural and healthy human desires. (Notice the words *bonding* and *developing* in the previous sentence. It's an ongoing endeavor.)

The purpose of this book it to lay out a plan that can help

you navigate the world of dating while avoiding many of the predictable pitfalls of romantic relationships in recovery.

While the challenges facing the recovering dater may be greater than they are for our nonaddicted "cousins," recovery principles are all about building relational skills. With practice, it's possible to enjoy dating while staying clean and sober—without feeling you're about to get voted off the island.

WHAT DO WE MEAN BY HEALTHY DATING?

First and foremost, healthy dating depends on staying clean and sober and working your program. It's a *process*, and you'll be hearing that word a lot throughout this book. Process means a gradual, developmental, progressive, methodical course of action. Another concept you'll become familiar with is *conscious choice*—meaning an aware, mindful, deliberate selection of options.

Principles of Twelve Step recovery provide information about your disease and offer suggestions on how to live happy, joyous, and free of addiction. The principles apply to everything in life, including dating and relating. Recovery works because it provides information and offers options for making healthy choices. The *Easy Does It Dating Guide* will use the same approach. It will provide information and suggestions; you'll have the opportunity to make conscious choices.

ACCEPTANCE: COMING TO GRIPS

The first stage of recovery is about accepting the disease of addiction and acquiring the skills to get along without alcohol, other drugs, or addictive behaviors. It's the first step of the journey toward greater awareness and finding your place in the world. For most people, early recovery provides the first experience of developing a meaningful relationship with self. It's a time of learning who you are and how you fit into the "tribe." Healthy dating begins with the relationship you form with yourself and your recovery community. No other relationships are possible until those are firmly in place.

Dating provides an opportunity to meet and spend time with people while learning more about who you are and exploring what it means to be in a relationship before actually committing to one. It's a trial time for learning how to make choices before emotional bonding takes place. Emotional bonding is the natural result of spending time together. It's an attachment you feel to a person you're attracted to that can quickly turn casual dating into compulsive relating—ready or not! It can keep you locked in unhealthy relationships even when you'd like to get out and move on. You'll read more about emotional bonding in the next chapter.

When the time is right, healthy dating follows the natural process of exploring deeper levels of intimacy. To make this journey without resorting to your addiction of choice, running for cover, or bolting for the door, you'll need a solid base of recovery and commitment to stay with your program. You need enough self-awareness to *know* who you are, boundaries to help you *stay* who you are, and the clarity to know if the relationship is what you *think* it is.

Suggested Prerequisites for Easy Does It Dating

Chances are you've experimented with "sport" dating. Early recovery is often filled with casual encounters that happen with little or no awareness on anyone's part, no real choices being made, and no commitment. These spur-of-the-moment affairs are a balm for early sobriety—taking the edge off the discomfort. They can also take the edge off recovery and are a primary cause for relapse.

It can take a year or longer and a few false starts before you make a full commitment to recovery. That's not wasted time; you're discovering important things about yourself. However, if you're still struggling with that early stage of recovery, you aren't ready to begin the dating process being presented in this book. Be good to yourself; read the book and save it for later.

The more time you spend focusing on yourself and learning how to live happy, joyous, and free—clean and sober— the better your chances of keeping those qualities when you get into a relationship. Twelve Step recovery is a lifelong course of action filled with self-discovery, leading to greater appreciation of your spiritual life. The likelihood of staying sober increases each year, rising sharply after five years, making that the ideal time frame for developing committed relationships. It's unlikely, however, that you'll wait that long before dating. In the first few years (yes, that's *years* not months), you've gotten a sneak peak into the package that is you; unpacking it is a long-term deal. Recovery is a process, life is a process, and ideally, dating is a process too.

RIGOROUS HONESTY

Okay, we just said five years was the *ideal*. Remember we're a people who seek progress not perfection. Let's imagine you have two years in recovery. Your relationship skills have been sharpening perhaps without you even being aware of it. It began when you put down your addictive substance, quit the using behavior, and began to get real. In meetings you've been practicing healthy communication—talking and listening respectfully to others. Working your way through the Steps is giving you insight, providing a formula for further social interaction. Working with your sponsor has jump-started the process of intimacy—sharing fears as well as hopes and dreams with another person. You want to begin dating, which is natural and a healthy sign that you're ready to get on with your life.

The following is a list of the qualities absolutely necessary for having a good dating experience—the "Easy Does It" way.

Checklist for a Healthy Dating Experience

1. ____ You have a solid base of recovery under your belt. (The suggested minimum is two years.)

During this time you have

2. ____ remained free of your addiction

3. ____ worked the Steps

4. ____ been meeting regularly with your sponsor (or have secured a dating sponsor—someone with whom you can discuss your thoughts, feelings, and experiences regarding dating)

5. ____ attended a home group regularly

A score of five means you can advance to the starting block. Four means proceed slowly and at your own risk. Three means you're headed for trouble. Two, one, or zero means keep coming back!

THE BUMP, BUMP, BUMPY ROAD TO LOVE

Whether you're addicted or not, whether you're a he looking for a she or a she looking for a he—or any combination of the above—and regardless of whether you're a freshman or a senior in life, you've probably had difficulties in the relationship department. Proof lies in the hundreds of dating books, thousands of my-lover-left-me, my-dog-died, and my-Chevy-won't-start blues, and the more than generous supply of soap operas groaning over love lost and love found only to be lost again.

Most therapists agree, however, that recovering people face specific challenges. Let's take a closer look at what you'll be bumping into as you begin dating. The good news is that regardless of what you encounter, your program provides solid guidelines for overcoming all difficulties. At times it can even put you a step ahead of the rest of the folks, but who's counting?

Traumatic Family History

Addiction is considered a "bio-psycho-social" disease. That's a fancy way of saying it affects body, mind, and spirit. *Bio* means biological, *psycho* means pertaining to the mind, and *social* refers to relationships. This section will primarily focus on the social factors, although all three factors are entwined and can't really be separated. Any discussion of these factors must begin with family, the effects of which shaped our core beings.

The myth of the "good" family has officially been put to rest. Experts estimate that between 80 and 96 percent of families qualify as dysfunctional. Dysfunction covers an assortment of circumstances ranging from severe abuse to benign neglect. And most of the problematic conditions are related to or directly caused by addiction. The potential for extreme abuse including violence is higher among families where addiction is actively being practiced than among the general population. This means if you come from an addictive family system, you are more apt to have difficulty in all areas of life—work, health, friendships, and committed relationships.

Good relationship skills depend on having basic emotional equipment up and running. If addiction was practiced in your home, it's likely your social skills are not fully developed. You probably aren't able to depend on your emotions when interacting with others. Your emotions can easily get distorted and play tricks on you. For some people this means being overly invested emotionally, and for others it means being emotionally guarded. The results of growing up in the environment being described means you often feel isolated, fearful, and unable to trust, or you don't know whom to trust.

Not everyone arrives in recovery with the same challenges. There are a lucky few who grew up in homes that provided a solid foundation. In those cases, addiction played only a minor part in the larger picture. These people usually have age-appropriate social skills, healthy beliefs about themselves, reasonably good values, and creative strategies for problem solving; socially they are up to speed. Recovery for them is a matter of quitting their addiction ("putting the plug in the jug"). Once they stop using, their lives return to normal. However, for most recovering people, this is not the case. Addiction has masked other problems that must be addressed.

Distorted Realities and Coping Skills

Dysfunctional families are wounded, and children from these families are survivors. In their struggle to find equilibrium, these children have often created a fantasy life that helps them endure. It's a protection against an intolerable reality they face every day. The most common survival mechanism in addiction is denial.

Denial is part of the addictive family profile that allows a child to tune out when the situation is too overwhelming. Later it becomes a way of looking at the world—blanking out what you don't want to see and seeing what you want to see—regardless of what is actually happening. It's impossible to make good decisions when denial is distorting your reality. In addition to the warped picture of the world, it blocks you from your authentic self and keeps you from having a real relationship with others. Denial often occurs through behaviors called *avoidance* and *romanticizing*.

Avoidance is a way of coping with past disappointment by shutting down hopes, dreams, and expectations. The avoider feels better having no desire at all than risking being disappointed again. Avoiders are armored against the world and even more so against close relationships. Often anger simmers beneath the calm surface, and there is the potential for violence. The violence might be expressed as emotional or physical attacks on another person or turned in against the self. Holding anger inside eventually leads to depression, despair, addiction, relapse, or suicide. Healthy relationships are based on communication and the ability to express mutual affection. Without recovery, avoidance makes intimate relationships impossible.

Romanticizing is like wearing rose-colored glasses—permanently. A line from an old song describes it clearly: "Falling in love with love is falling for make-believe." The romantic paints her world the way she wants it to be and falls in love with her creation. Disconnected from reality, she has no discernment. She is as apt to "fall in love" with an inappropriate partner as an appropriate one. If her fantasy includes living happily ever after, she'll stay to the end no matter what. It is possible to die of romance by staying in abusive situations until death literally does the parting.

As If That's Not Enough . . .

Emotional immaturity: Emotional development comes screeching to a halt when addiction activates. During recovery, you begin developing where you left off—meaning there is often a teenager or even a much younger part of yourself that surfaces during the first stages. Often childhood has been delayed by taking on adult responsibilities—filling in for immature or absent parents. The child within has never learned to be a kid—to let go, play, and experience simply being. Luckily, recovery works like dog years, and it doesn't take a whole twelve months to grow a year. However, early recovery is an adjustment time—the first two to three years are basically about catching up. Dating heaps more pressure on an already stressful situation.

The "immediate gratification gene": This is that rambunctious little bit of DNA lurking in the bio-chemical makeup of the addicted—if not in reality, at least figuratively. The suggested time delay for beginning to date in recovery is two years—and that is the *bare minimum.* However, that impetuous genetic material is shouting in your ear that "time's a-wasting," so there's no guarantee you'll wait. If you do decide that you must get out of the recovery boat and push the river before the recommended time, you will most likely be consulting the "Breaking Up: Damage Control" chapter before you really want to. Having a dating plan can help you keep that from happening.

"I'm different," or terminal uniqueness: Whether this is a story we addictive people tell ourselves so we can feel special or whether we actually are as unique as we seem to think we are hasn't been officially proven. Just how much the I'm-different factor enters into the dating picture hasn't been formally determined either. Dating and not drinking

or drugging, however, is definitely a different experience for most of us, and it's going to require some unique approaches. If not unique, at least it's true to say that many recovering folks are notorious rebels. However, this can be an asset when it comes to not following the crowd when it's going a direction you've already been.

Fuzzy Math: When Two Halves Don't Make a Whole

Codependency can be described as when yesterday's survival skills get in the way of today's healthy relationships. Codependency isn't a definitive term as much as a catchall for symptoms that result from addiction and growing up in homes where addiction or other dysfunctional parenting was the norm. Often these patterns have characterized family relationships for generations. They have a negative effect on all aspects of relating—affecting self-image, communication, and the ability to give and receive love.

Codependency begins as a coping strategy and becomes an effective means of surviving intolerable conditions. Melody Beattie, author and pioneer in the field of codependency, characterizes the pattern as "sneaky," "deceptive," and "progressive." In adulthood these adaptive behaviors become maladaptive—making healthy relationships impossible. It takes time to heal damaged self-esteem and to learn new behaviors such as setting and holding boundaries, feeling and expressing emotions, problem solving in healthy ways, and most of all, learning to love yourself and others. It's a healing process that goes on for many years.

Codependent behaviors can be broadly understood as two systems that are really different sides of the same coin; both get in the way of successful relationships. Codependency shows up as overinvolvement with others; "counter-dependency," its flip side, appears as being overly independent.

Codependents are more aware of what's going on around

them than what's going on inside them. They habitually disregard their own needs to take care of others. Having little in the way of self-worth, the feeling of not being enough drives them to seek completion through others—compulsively doing for someone else. (Service work is the keystone of recovery but has to be balanced with learning how to take care of yourself.) The codependent's motto might be "You need and therefore I am."

Counter-dependency is independency to a fault—appearing to be self-contained, secure, not needing anyone. In practice the counter-dependent appears indifferent, accepting the attention and favors of others while giving very little back. In reality the counter-dependent, like his mirror twin the codependent, has poor self-esteem. He often teams up with a codependent and absorbs the partner to make himself seem bigger and more powerful. The counter-dependent's motto might be "I am therefore you need." It takes two to tango, and it's a deadly dance.

Ah! At last, my other half! But two halves don't make a whole when it comes to human relationships. Two wounded people desperately searching for someone else to fill the void isn't a relationship; it's a guaranteed train wreck. The trick is that it feels so right—for a while—but it's a recipe for chronic discontent. Your other half never performs exactly the way you would if you were the other half.

The truth is, each half is searching for a part of the self that's hidden inside. The codependent has power he's afraid of owning. The counter-dependent has a vulnerable softer side she keeps safely locked behind her walls. Recovery is about developing our own missing halves—and going into the world feeling whole. Healthy relationships are accomplished by two whole people *choosing* to be with each other not out of need but out of interest that eventually can ripen into love. (You can find additional resources on codependency and other behaviors that accompany addiction in the suggested readings found in appendix B.)

In truth, very few recovering people wait the estimated five to seven years that it takes for recovery principles to be firmly in place before seeking a relationship. With the support and structure of your program and a dating plan based in recovery principles, you can work your program as you go. Always remember, though, that it takes a high level of commitment, personal awareness, and continued vigilance to stay on course.

RELATIONSHIP HELL: DATING TRAPS YOU CAN AVOID

The beauty of recovery meetings is that you don't personally have to make all the mistakes in the book. You've heard the saying that you can take the elevator all the way to the basement or get off at the mezzanine. With that in mind, let's take a look at what others have learned in the dating process with the hopes of sparing you an unnecessary trip to the cellar— or an unexpected visit to Dante's Inferno. Of course everyone reserves the right to get off at the floor (or circle) of choice. This book promotes personal preference, and yours will be respected throughout the following pages. Here's a list of common traps; perhaps you have some to add to it.

Taking or Being Taken Hostage

The hostage situation happens when you pressure or coerce your partner into a relationship, and when he wants to get out, you refuse to let go, making him your emotional prisoner. Remember, successful agreements move ahead slowly; be sure to establish clear ground rules as you go, including an exit strategy.

The Velcro Syndrome

This describes a relationship where you think you can't live without the other. This is a scratchy kind of relationship that's irritating and downright sticky regardless of which role you play—clinger or clung to.

Some Day My Prince(ss) Will Come . . .

This describes the wait-and-see-who-will-rescue-me kind of relationship. Like Sleeping Beauty with her hundred-year nap, you have no real life without your prince (or princess) charming. Or like the little green frog perched on his lily pad awaiting the kiss of his princess, you run the risk of croaking before your real life begins.

Undercover Lover

This man in black or mysterious veiled woman reeks of intrigue, plays footsie under the table, but never lets on that you're together. The undercover lover never introduces you to anyone and is apt to disappear into a crowd and not come back for days—make that years.

Fixer-Uppers

Fixer-uppers are those poor souls you bring home to soak in your bathtub while you read your latest self-help book to them. Your life turns into a series of personal seminars on Shoe Tying 101, while you wonder why these ingrates aren't thanking you for "everything you did for them."

Legal High

This person goes from flower to flower getting drunk on the heady nectar of first love. The attraction has nothing to do with you; you are simply the catalyst for the chemicals to keep the buzz buzzing. A couple of good stiff "sniffs" and he'll be gone.

The Fantasia Fix

You are the screen upon which another projects a love fantasy. Like the Legal High, it has nothing to do with you. Regardless of which side of the drama you are on—the projector or the screen—it is not going to be a good movie.

Telling: All or Nothing at All

Telling all is when you confuse personal sharing with going to confession. The opposite includes keeping secrets when you should share information, such as when you're contagious—including anything from a cold to a sexually transmitted disease.

SUMMARY POINTS

- Dating and forming a bond with another person is a natural, healthy human desire.
- Healthy dating is a process that begins with you getting to know yourself.
- The road to dating in recovery has bumps, and program principles will help you over them.
- Dating is *never* an excuse for using.

Next you'll read about the progressive steps to building a relationship and what to expect as you go. We'll also begin applying recovery principles to dating and relating—increasing your odds for success.

Chapter Two

Dating: A Need or "Amuck"?

- What's spirituality have to do with it?
- From love limbo to single—*it's a real life!*
- Intimacy and commitment begin at home.
- We never outgrow our need for the Serenity Prayer.

Sometimes we're afraid to admit what it is we really want. And most of us don't know the difference between natural needs and desires and addiction rearing its ugly head. As you've learned in recovery, all addictions are rooted in basic human instincts run amuck. *Recovery is about knowing the difference between a need and "amuck."*

Self-determination is the ability to decide what you want and go after it, and it is a mark of a well-developed person. Recovery holds the promise of happiness, joy, and freedom and gives us the very real opportunity of developing self-determination and having those promises come true.

The position taken in this book is that dating and having a romantic relationship with another person is a natural human instinct and is something most people will seek. Healthy dating begins as you make conscious choices about what's important to you and take steps toward your goal. When it comes to relationships, it takes a sufficient degree of self-awareness to recognize when instinct morphs into addiction and when "amuck" lurks around the next corner. *Remember, you've got a framework in which to operate, a supportive community behind you, and a natural desire. You can do this!*

FROM OZZIE AND HARRIET TO OZZY AND SHARON

Our understanding of dating, relating, and marriage has changed radically over the last half century since Ozzie and Harriet gave way to Ozzy and Sharon. The women's movement of the '60s and '70s presented new options to society. The advent of the birth control pill brought family planning into the mainstream. Increased educational opportunities opened careers, granting economic freedom for many women beyond anything their mothers or grandmothers could have imagined. As a result, greater numbers began placing career ahead of the traditional occupation of homemaker and mother, delaying marriage, or opting to remain single. Those who married became less likely to remain in unsatisfactory or abusive marriages.

New forms of commitment have entered the mainstream, many people are delaying marriage, and more are opting to not marry at all. Today, nearly half of the adult workforce is made up of singles—a huge shift from a generation ago.

What people expect out of relationships and matrimony has changed too. Today both men and women look for love, romance, security, trust, sexual fulfillment, spiritual and psychological growth, happiness, commitment, friendship, communication, shared interests, as well as a satisfying family life—a much longer list than a generation ago when people just wanted to raise their kids!

Forever: Not As Long As It Used to Be

People no longer expect a relationship to last forever; this includes marriage and other committed unions. For better or for worse, for richer or for poorer, serial monogamy is becoming the norm in how we think about partnering. This means more people are going to be living greater portions of their lives as singles. And they will be doing so at intervals throughout their adult years.

One result of this reconfiguration is a new understanding of the single state. In generations past, being single was time spent waiting for marriage. For women, the closer it came to that culturally imposed cutoff age of twenty-five, the more hand-wringing that went on at family gatherings. Men had a slight advantage as bachelors. Suspicion eventually surfaced somewhere in a man's midthirties, spawning the rhetorical question, "Isn't it about time you settled down?"

Seasons and Cycles of Life

On the average, most of us will live into our early eighties. Many of us will easily reach our nineties, but let's settle for eighty-five. If what the experts say is true, our relationships will cycle through the same essential segments many times over a lifetime. We'll be single, date, bond, form a committed relationship, go through some form of dissolution, and return again to spend time as a single person. Each cycle brings the opportunity to grow in self-understanding, truly know another person, and explore what it means to love.

Almost everyone who arrives in recovery has experienced an ending—referred to in program talk as "bottoming out." This involves grieving at some level. You might be one of the many teens and young adults whose early onset of addiction interrupted normal developmental processes, and you grieve for those lost experiences. You grieve for the childhood you never had and for the loss of the drugs and behaviors that were a salve to those wounds. You grieve for what you think is the end of the good times. You might be newly divorced or emerging from a breakup of some kind of partnership, and you grieve for the broken promises.

Grief leads to introspection. Your recovery program takes you through Steps that help you learn what makes you tick. You unlock patterns that kept you a prisoner of self-defeating behaviors and learn how to do it differently. Most of all, you meet your Higher Power (H.P.) and realize your innate self-worth. Rather than love limbo, being single is a time of deep transformation.

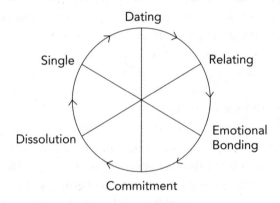

STAGE ONE: SINGLE—IT'S A REAL LIFE!

For many people, ideas about marriage have changed, and ideas about being single have too. Concepts and words such as *family of origin, inner child,* and *self-healing* have crept into the culture. The recovery movement and the prominence of Twelve Step communities helped to introduce spirituality to the world of self-help. The concepts have become mainstream, making self-awareness, healing, and spirituality regular topics for discussion on television, in movies, and in books, giving us plenty to ponder on those nights alone by the fire. Gradually the concept of being single shifted from time spent in between lives—a limbo for the loveless—to single as a *real life*.

The new understanding of single doesn't emphasize the individual at the expense of belonging in a community. It recognizes the spiritual importance of knowing who you are as a person and choosing your place in the community.

* * *

Stage One: Single—It's a Real Life!
Single is a time of stabilizing your sobriety, working the Steps with a sponsor, going to meetings, and being with friends. It's a time of self-discovery.

- Intimacy: involves bonding with self
- Commitment: comes through showing up consistently in recovery
- Skills:
  * Self-awareness through Step work
  * Self-care through learning boundaries
  * Self-love through developing your spirituality

* * *

Intimacy and commitment form the basis for all our relationships. They aren't items to be checked off like a grocery list but have to be firmly built into self-awareness. You will draw on them for the rest of your life. Intimacy for the single person in recovery is about discovering who you are, and commitment is about consistently "showing up" in your recovery. This inner bond has to be established before any other relationship can happen.

Whether you are new to the single scene or a seasoned solo, recovery is a time of increased self-discovery and healing. It's a chance to put your attention on your program and to enjoy the fellowship. It offers you the freedom to pursue your interests without having to consider anyone else in your plans. While this may not be as true if your life includes children, being single can provide you with more freedom to think of yourself than if you were with a partner. It's a time to consider career choices, further your education, and explore other ways of developing your talents. It's also a time to work on your social skills, make new friends, and eventually expand into new circles. Being single and in recovery also provides the opportunity to learn how to be with others and to be of service to your community.

STAGE TWO: SINGLE AND DATING

Let's imagine the day has arrived for you to add dating to your life as a single person. You're going to keep thinking and acting like a single person. You'll continue your self-discovery, learning more about yourself through interacting with another person. Your intimacy bond remains within yourself, and your commitment to recovery is still your primary focus. *If either of those two things gets compromised, the deal is off!*

* * *

Stage Two: Single and Dating
You've bonded to yourself and know how to keep yourself safe. Now you're putting all you've learned into practice—testing your skills while being true to yourself (staying you) while dating. This includes spending brief periods of time with different people, while remaining free of emotional or sexual entanglement (shopping but not buying).

- Intimacy: learning more about self
- Commitment: staying true to self

- Skills:
  * Holding your boundaries (you are you and the other is the other)
  * Making conscious choices
  * Practicing social skills
  * Learning how to feel comfortable and safe
  * Learning how to move on
  * *Having fun!*

Remember, we are presenting the ideal. Like every other aspect of recovery, it's going to include mistakes, otherwise known as learning experiences. The ideal includes making conscious choices and testing your ability to set and hold boundaries while spending time with another. It's an opportunity to meet new people and apply your social skills—keeping your interactions light, friendly, and positive. You'll also have a chance to practice moving on *before* emotional attachment occurs—walking away on your own two feet rather than being carried off the field.

Your job is to practice being comfortable, feeling safe, and having fun. You might enjoy this phase of dating for several years, seeing as many different people as possible. You'll avoid emotional entanglement by not dating anyone more than a few times. Terence Gorski, relationship guru and therapist, believes that learning how to break up is as important as learning how to get along. He recommends going through the process of dating and breaking up with at least six people before settling into a relationship with one particular person.

Many people in recovery find walking away to be extremely difficult and might want to work additional recovery programs such as Co-dependents Anonymous (CoDA), Adult Children of Alcoholics (ACA), or others.

And what if you believe you've found the "right one" on your first or second date? Recovering people are more likely than nonrecovering people to become emotionally attached too early, increasing the likelihood of falling into an unhealthy dependency or addiction (settling for Mr. or Ms. Right Now rather than Mr. or Ms. Right On). If you feel you have really found the right one, it won't hurt to continue dating others and go through the steps in this chapter. As difficult as this sounds (and *is*), the point of following a dating plan is to make sure you are selecting a partner, not falling into a trap that has more to do with addiction than making a conscious choice.

There isn't any time limit on the single and dating stage of the process; it can last for a year, two years, or longer. If you're having fun, by all means wait awhile before actively looking for a partner. You can move to the next level when it feels right, as long as it isn't too soon.

Stage Three: Selecting a Partner

Let's say you've gotten good at the skills described in the earlier stages and are ready to consider letting your dating begin to move toward relating. Attraction to another person and shared values make the best combination for a successful partnership. Attraction readily makes itself known, *but it takes time to observe values.* The emphasis on moving slowly is designed to increase your chances of getting to the point of partner selection with someone who *has* the essential qualities you are seeking—not someone who just *says* he has them or someone who you think *might* learn them. (In chapter 7 you'll find suggestions on discovering your best qualities and also how to identify what's important to you in a partner.) Partner selection means you are checking people out to see how well they match your preferences. By dating a variety of people, you're learning how to be selective.

You'll be checking in regularly with your sponsor to make sure you're holding the line and staying true to what you said you wanted. Most likely you'll do some adjusting to your expectations and priorities, discovering things you are attracted to in the other person you hadn't even thought of. However, it's just as likely you'll be tempted to adjust the bar, either raising or lowering it. Recovering people tend to be at one end or the other of the spectrum: either too willing to settle or impossible to please. It's good to sound things out with someone. Again, the choices are yours. Talking with others helps you stay true to yourself. Partner selection can take a few months or a few years, and you can be very attracted to someone and discover the relationship isn't right for you. It takes a strong commitment to yourself and the willingness to stay with your truth.

* * *

Stage Three: Selecting a Partner

Partner selection ideally begins before emotional bonding or sex happens. That's how you can make a conscious choice. You'll be working with the information you've been gathering about the qualities that are important to you.

- Intimacy: remains within yourself.
- Commitment: is still to you and your recovery; it involves sharing with friends and your sponsor. You are committed to staying present and making conscious choices. Willingness to be true to the ideals you've established is necessary for you in a relationship. No selling out or settling!

- Skills:
    * Self-honesty and integrity to stay with your truth
    * Enough flexibility and openness to let your Higher Power add something new you hadn't thought of
    * Enough self-knowledge to know whether you're in over your head or just scared
    * Ability to negotiate boundaries
    * Willingness to move on if things aren't right for you

In a perfect world you would then be ready for stage four, moving from dating to relating, but sex, love, and attachment all live close together in the bio-chemical and psychological systems of the addicted. You're going to need all the skills you've been building, as well as some new ones, as you enter the deeper stages of relationships.

STAGE FOUR: FROM DATING TO RELATING

The shift from dating to relating happens gradually as you find yourself attracted to someone and that someone is attracted back. At this point, nature steps in and quickly becomes more in control of the process than we are. Emotional bonding begins simply by being with someone and by beginning to share feelings. Sharing feelings makes you vulnerable, and it's good to be reminded that emotional vulnerability always carries a risk, making this phase of dating a bit like walking a tightrope.

Let's face it. Probably no one has ever done vulnerability exactly right. You'll have questions. How emotionally open is too open? What is too protective? How selective is selective enough? When does being selective cross the line into avoidance? Again, these are all issues best resolved by talking with your sponsor and friends and in prayer and meditation. You'll get the guidance you need by staying connected to your own inner process.

* * *

Stage Four: From Dating to Relating

The shift from dating to relating is yet another process. It's the beginning of emotional bonding. Having it happen with the right person is the intended payoff of your careful step-by-step choice making.

- Intimacy: now includes another person as well as you, and you both need to remain true to yourself and your recovery. You'll begin sharing feelings with each other, and it's an exciting and "intoxicating" time in your relationship. Success depends on staying with your spiritual practice and talking with your sponsor.
- Commitment: still remains within yourself as you gradually assess your potential partner's qualities and shortcomings as well as your own. You're taking on balancing another person's hopes, dreams, and expectations with yours, checking to see if the relationship works and if you can handle the extra emotional contact.
- Skills:
  * Ability to feel your feelings and share them
  * Enough personal development or maturity to stay in conversations without jumping to conclusions
  * Respect and sensitivity to self and other
  * Good communication and conflict-resolution skills
  * Ability to balance your schedule to accommodate another person without giving yourself away or keeping the other away

* * *

Being in a relationship takes considerable time and energy. Be realistic about what you can and cannot do. Your addictive relationships had an all-or-nothing quality, so finding the balance point for each of you is a necessary and important part of deciding whether to move ahead. People have different ideas and needs regarding time, and these usually don't change unless making adjustments becomes a priority to both parties. As in the previous stage, you might get to this point in your relationship and find things aren't working out as well as you thought they would—or that you aren't doing as well as you'd like to be doing. There aren't any hard-and-fast rules on any part of the process, but you might consider giving it six months to a year to see if all the basics line up and if you both feel ready to move on to stage five.

Stage Five: Committed Relationship

At this stage, you're feeling the fun, excitement, and passion that go with love. Sexual intimacy will no doubt enter the picture, and you'll need to deal with the practical side of matters. You've settled the question of *who* you are committing to, and now there's the question of *what* you are committing to. It's important to talk things through together, finding out what each of you wants and needs to feel safe and comfortable in a sexual relationship. Exploring expectations takes time and new questions arise as you go, making good communication a necessity.

If you're talking about monogamy, spell out exactly what that means. If either of you expect a formal commitment, such as engagement or marriage, either now or in the future, the conversation needs to happen before sexuality begins. It's better to risk having that talk now than discovering later that you have different ideas about the future. (There's more on sexual intimacy in chapter 8.)

Stage Five: Committed Relationship

As you decide to move into a committed relationship, the level of intimacy increases and so does the complexity. Good, honest, and open communication is needed as expectations and definitions of intimacy, commitment, monogamy, and what the future may or may not hold need to be clearly stated and agreed on. It's good to recognize that *feeling* like you can't live without someone doesn't mean that you *actually* can't live without that person.

- Intimacy: involves deep emotional sharing, preparing for a sexual relationship, and considering the possibility of building a life together
- Commitment: includes a deepening on all levels— to self and continued recovery, to your partner, and to the relationship
- Skills include everything you've learned so far plus an increase in the following abilities:
  * To trust
  * To love and be loved
  * To negotiate, including arguing
  * To forgive and forget
  * To continue building your sense of self

* * *

The traditional time for engagement, if that is where your relationship is headed, is after being together for six months to a year. Many people make this level of commitment only once and spend the rest of their lives with their partner. Despite what the statistics indicate, forever is still the ideal picture for many of us. If forever is important to both you and your partner, the process presented here will give you the best chance of success.

STAGE SIX: LEAVING, GRIEVING, AND HEALING

Regardless of careful planning, there are times when a couple can't move the relationship to the next level. When this happens the connection usually breaks—seldom into two exactly even pieces. Usually one person wants to end the relationship, and the other wants to continue it. It takes both people signing on to make a go of it. If either one can't or won't, the relationship ends. The one who leaves often bears the pain of guilt; the one who is left feels the pain of rejection.

* * *

Stage Six: Leaving, Grieving, and Healing
This stage can happen anywhere during the relationship if expectations aren't mutual and commitment can't be agreed upon.

- Intimacy: develops into a stronger bond with self and with spiritual source; includes sharing of self with friends, family, and recovering community
- Commitment: transfers back to self and deepens
- Skills:
  * Grieving: allow yourself to go through the process of feeling the loss.
  * Allowing your feelings to be what they are: some days you'll feel just great, and other times you'll feel down.
  * Healing: there is a natural healing that happens by staying with your process. Sometimes additional counseling helps.

* Rediscovering self: you'll find new strengths and
  also new vulnerabilities.
* Transforming self: a complete change will happen
  when you stay with the process rather than engaging in addictive behavior or jumping into another
  relationship too soon.

* * *

Breaking up is difficult and is a potentially dangerous
place for anyone in recovery. The newly sober seldom survive. This is why taking time before moving ahead in the
process and attempting a committed relationship is so
strongly emphasized. You need strength, good recovery,
and particular skills to survive any crisis. If a breakup happens, the goal of this book is to help you land on both feet
clean and sober when it's over. After a time of grieving,
even the deepest wounds have the potential to turn into the
greatest strengths—if only to tell you that you don't want to
do it the same way again.

You've gotten a look at the big picture and know where
this book is going. Each of these stages will be examined in
detail later on, but first let's see how you can avail yourself
of the most powerful benefit of recovery, using it to launch
into your relationship venture.

A Moment of Silence Followed by the Serenity Prayer

There are loads of seminars and books devoted to dating
and mating. Why not simply pick one and use it? They're
good, but they don't always translate into recovery principles and don't take advantage of one of the most important things you have going: making conscious contact with
your Higher Power. Applying spiritual principles to your

clean-and-sober dating plan can provide the edge needed to make it work. To advance this theory, let's turn to the tried-and-true Serenity Prayer (sometimes referred to as the national anthem of recovery). Following is a slightly altered version of the prayer, adapted to illustrate this point (with thanks, of course, to Dr. Reinhold Niebuhr who composed the original).

God, grant me the serenity
To be in a healthy relationship,
Accepting myself and the other person for who we are,
The willingness to hold the line or
Change my expectations when appropriate and
The wisdom to know the difference.

Now let's take the real version line-by-line to help get the process started.

God, grant me the serenity: Beginning with the first word of this prayer, you see you aren't in this thing alone. You have the option of making conscious contact with your Higher Power *before* proceeding. Hopefully you've begun to experience your relationship with your Higher Power in a loving way.

Serenity has been described in many different ways: the freedom from worry, experiencing inner peace on a regular basis, feeling stress free, and being free of disturbing thoughts. Serenity carries an abiding sense that life is unfolding according to plans not entirely of one's own making but in one's best interest. When trouble pops up as it does throughout life, serenity is that quality that assures us we will be given the strength to endure, even transcend, our circumstances.

While it takes more than a few years to embody serenity, by now you've probably caught the flavor of it—and you want more. In program talk it's the I-want-what-you-have-and-I'm-willing-to-go-to-any-length-to-get-it stuff you've heard about. Serenity helps you make good choices in all areas of life by prompting you to ask this question: Will my choice increase my serenity or jeopardize it?

To accept the things I cannot change: You may not be as familiar with the concept of acceptance as you are with its opposite—the immediate gratification gene mentioned in the first chapter. Acceptance got you here, and without it you would be reading something else right now like *Speed Dating!* However, you're here reading the *Easy Does It Dating Guide: For People in Recovery.* You could be in worse shape.

Here are a few suggestions regarding acceptance you might want to consider before venturing into the dating world.

Regardless of how many times we say the word *process,* you're going to hear *fast-forward.* You'll say to yourself a hundred times, "What's the point of all this process? Let's get this thing bagged!" Time will feel like your enemy—like someone or something might go wrong. This translates into the fear of losing control. And at the exact nanosecond your dating plan appears to be remotely working, you'll probably get scared, and that same fear of losing control will cause you to stall.

Acceptance includes realizing that the model for relationships you carry around in your head probably isn't a healthy one. In all likelihood you lack the emotional footing you need to recognize a healthy relationship—even if it bites you on the toe. Addicted parents taught you as best they could about relationships; however, their primary relationship was with their drug of choice. Everyone (you) and everything else (your needs) took second place. If you're reading this book, you've mastered many survival skills, but you're probably still short on the relational ones. But like the map in the mall that says "You are here," once you accept where you are, you can get anywhere you want to go—*and this time you have help.*

The courage to change the things I can: You've already *changed* the belief that you had to use addictively to live and *"ex-changed"* much of the misery that went with using. You're becoming comfortable (some of the time) in your skin. Life is opening up, a change from the shrinking world of addiction. The good news—the really good news—is that despite the string of broken relationships in your past, you now have a program that's teaching you Step by Step how to do it differently. It begins with knowing who you are, grows into loving who you are, and eventually guides you in finding someone with whom to share this love. Recovery is a process of stripping away layers of false beliefs. It eventually lets you realize that maybe God knew what she was doing when she designed you.

And the wisdom to know the difference: Wisdom is life experience plus spiritual insight multiplied by years. There just isn't a shortcut. Wisdom mulches experiences, eventually turning even our worst mess into fertile soil for growing something new. Wisdom takes into account personal challenges as well as talents, factoring them into the limitations of being human, and comes up with a favorable number. It's loaded with forgiveness.

Wisdom is why children sidle up to old people and lean into them. Children sense the stability and love. We find wisdom in recovery through sharing stories and sponsorship. The truly wise hardly ever tell you what to do or not do; they realize the value of living it. They might tell you what they learned along the way, and the smart person listens, taking the lessons and using them. If you don't, it's okay too. Wisdom won't hold experience against you. Life is a series of happenings; learn to relax, enjoy, and find the love as you go.

Putting a Few Relationship Myths to Rest

We all grew up with the same fairy-tale ideas about relationships. These ideas came from our families, movies, books, television, and sometimes plain old wishful thinking. Here are some common misunderstandings about the nature of relationships, each followed by a more realistic understanding:

Myth: Being single is what happens when you aren't in a relationship.

Truth: Being single is a real life—whole and complete unto itself. Some people choose to remain single and others choose to be single for a time before re-entering the dating scene and before making further commitment to someone else. Making conscious choices means you can determine what is right for you, and you can change your mind when your process lets you know it's time to change.

Myth: Dating is something to "get through" until you find someone.

Truth: Dating can be an interesting and exciting opportunity to learn new skills, meet new people, and expand into new social circles. Landing a date isn't an end in itself, and no one is keeping score unless you are. It's all about your attitude. If you find you need an attitude adjustment to make your dating life more fun, remember, this is the *Easy Does It Dating Guide.* Just kick back and read it all before heading out.

Myth: When a relationship "fails," I'm a failure.

Truth: When a relationship ends, it doesn't always have to be someone's fault. Relationships have three components—you, the other person, and the relationship. Usually more than one of the three parts have malfunctioned. If you really feel you have brought on the failure of a relationship through faulty behavior, you have the choice of labeling yourself a failure or doing some work to make things right. Making things right doesn't always mean staying or going back; it can mean taking responsibility for your behavior and making amends (think Tenth Step).

Myth: When the going gets tough, it's time to go.

Truth: All relationships go through hard times. Sometimes trouble can mean getting help and trying harder, and other times it can mean letting go. Depending on your religious or cultural background, whether children are involved, and other reasons, you may find that a greater ethic is served by staying in a relationship even when you'd like to get out. If that is the case, you'll be given the grace to stay. You'll grow spiritually and eventually find new levels of happiness. Ask anyone who has made it into the double digits as a couple, and they'll tell you that hanging in there when the going gets tough has its own reward.

Myth: Love conquers all.

Truth: Love is a choice. There are choices that lead you to love's doorway and choices about stepping through it to the other side. Making good, clear decisions beginning with the ones you make as a single, nondating person, as well as those made while dating, increase the odds of a really wonderful love match. The love-conquers-all approach smacks of magical thinking that isn't going to serve you or the object of your affection well in the long run.

Myth: My soul mate will drop down my chimney and find me.

Truth: No, Virginia, that's Santa Claus. Would you really want to date somebody who dropped down your chimney?

Myth: There is one certain person just for me.

Truth: Maybe. But it's more likely there are many different people you could be with, love, and be loved by. The only-one-for-me belief limits your options. What if you're away on vacation when that certain someone stops by your desk? This myth is imbued with romanticism, and romanticism doesn't mix well with making conscious choices—which includes choosing your beliefs.

SUMMARY POINTS

- Single is a *real life* whether or not you choose to be in a relationship.
- Recovery has transferable skills and spiritual benefits that can be applied to your dating venture.
- Life offers a cycle of relationships—with self, family, friends, community, and eventually a partner. We may find ourselves revisiting the cycle throughout a lifetime, giving us the opportunity to grow and learn.

- After a time of grieving, even the deepest
  wounds have the potential to turn into the greatest
  strengths—if only to tell you that you don't want to
  do it the same way again.

We'd all choose to do better in relationships if we could. In the next chapter you'll see how taking another Fourth Step can bring more insight and freedom from subconscious patterns that seem to thwart even your best efforts. Let's face it. Nobody wants to drag this stuff around forever!

Chapter Three *

Getting Different Results

- Getting to the root of the problem.
- Transforming and healing through ceremony.
- Unlocking the power of your truth.
- Trudge, trudge, trudge that "Road to Happy Destiny"!

Despite the occasional stories to the contrary, a job rarely floats in the window, a school seldom calls asking us to register, and an apartment drops in our lap only once in a blue moon. In reality, we have to go through the process of looking for work, school, or a place to live. The same is true of dating. Sometimes we hesitate to actively seek a partner because our unhealthy relationship history has left us unsure of ourselves. We're not sure what's normal and what's being fanned by the fires of addiction. Healthy dating is about taking responsibility, and this means making conscious choices and actively seeking the things we want and need. Recovery is a program of action and the Steps guide the way.

Housekeeping: Taking the Fourth (Again)

If you haven't had a successful relationship history, you'll want to find out why. Your program Step work has helped you to discover many hidden beliefs that kept you locked in self-defeating patterns. Taking another Fourth Step specifically on past romantic relationships will reveal even more helpful information. Our beliefs about ourselves—our desirability, what we believe we deserve, as well as perceptions about our abilities—are based on our experiences of the past. If your experiences were healthy, there's no problem; if they were unhealthy, they can unconsciously sabotage you, causing even your best efforts to fail. Another Fourth Step brings more hidden assumptions to awareness, allowing more conscious choices. As you will discover, *conscious choices* is the *Easy Does It Dating Guide* theme song.

Making Conscious Connections

For this Fourth Step you'll apply the same method you used when taking the Fourth Step in your Twelve Step program, using the slightly modified form below. You'll be working across the page in nine columns, so you might want to tape several pieces of paper together.

1. List your past significant romantic relationships.
2. Identify what was going on in your life just prior to each relationship. What was happening and what were you feeling? (For example, I just moved to Podunk, and I was feeling lonely. Or I just lost my job and was feeling really stupid about myself.)
3. If sex was part of the relationship, how long did you know this person before becoming sexual together?
4. How long did the relationship last?
5. What feelings did you have during this relationship?
6. Who ended it and why?
7. What were your feelings when it ended?
8. How did you handle your feelings?

9. How long before you got into the next significant romantic relationship?

When you have answered these questions regarding all past significant relationships, go over the results with your dating sponsor or another person you trust. This isn't about whether you've been naughty or nice but about uncovering self-defeating patterns. As you go over the results, look for connections, including

- your emotional condition prior to each relationship
- expectations as you entered each relationship
- feelings that dominated each relationship
- how each relationship ended
- feelings you were left with
- beliefs you hold about yourself and about relation-ships that were reinforced by the relationship and the breakup

Analyzing Your Results

Using the following list as a guide, analyze your inventory:

- List the feelings you discovered. Find one or two that are the most intense. Sit quietly and ask your-self how far back these feelings go.
- What were the underlying (hidden) needs you had going into each relationship?
- Did you make conscious choices throughout the relationship or was there something you "knew" about yourself, the other person, or the nature of the relationship that you hid from yourself?
- What have you learned about yourself?
- What are your strengths?
- What are your vulnerabilities?

- What behaviors or feelings do you want repeated
  in your next relationship?
- What behaviors or feelings are you definitely elimi-
  nating from the next relationship?

Some insights come quickly, and others surface gradually. Give yourself enough time to get to the bottom line. For
example, insecurity isn't the bottom line; many people are
insecure. Ask yourself what you are insecure about. What
is underneath the insecurity? For example, you might be
afraid or ashamed that you are not enough, are unlovable,
or are permanently flawed. A Fourth Step brings greater self-
awareness and allows more healing.

Letting Go with Love

As you look back over the assumptions you've made about
life and relationships, see if they are rooted in your childhood experiences. When you look at your beliefs through
the eyes of the child, you'll see they make sense according
to your experiences in early life. The coping behaviors you
developed are rational and understandable when you see
them from a child's point of view. Eventually you'll find a
particular belief about yourself or about life that weaves its
way through everything. Validate it; there is a reason for it.
Something happened to cause it.

When you accept that the decisions and choices you
made in the past were as good as they could be at that time,
it frees you to believe you can make good choices now. If
you keep second-guessing yourself, putting yourself down,
or trying to protect others, you can't heal. It's time to tell
your side of the story, your truth. If there were times when
those who were supposed to take care of you failed, whether
they did it intentionally or through circumstances beyond
their control, *you got hurt.* You've probably been reacting

ever since. This may be the first time the "kid" in you has had the chance to tell it from her side. This isn't the time to forgive or understand things from others' perspectives. That comes later as the result of healing.

The following story shows how Lisa gained important insight by getting to her truth about the events of her life. She was then able to let it go with love for herself and the others involved.

Lisa finished her Fourth Step and discovered her fear of abandonment was a thread running through all her relationships. Below it was a worse fear that she was not lovable—unworthy to the core. It shaped her behavior in every relationship. As she dug further into her history, she remembered the family stories about her birth. Her mother was sick when Lisa was born. Rather than immediately being placed in her mother's arms as is the traditional practice, she was hurried away to the hospital nursery where she spent most of her first five days. Of course she was taken care of in the nursery, but the early bonding she needed with her mother didn't happen. The separation continued when they went home. Interaction with her mother was kept to a minimum, and other family members cared for her. The separation was done to protect her, but it resulted in a deep psychological wound she felt throughout her life.

In junior high she discovered alcohol and boys—the perfect fix for her insecurity, until it became the problem. She consistently made bad choices in her relationships—meaning no choices. If a boy showed any interest in her, she was like a lost puppy following him around—doing anything to avoid being abandoned—which usually included sex anywhere, anytime. Of course, exactly what she feared happened in almost every case: she abandoned herself and was continually used and discarded. She escaped into alcohol and drugs to numb her emotional pain, further abandoning herself. Like most addicted people, Lisa came into recovery angry at the world. Without insight into what was beneath the anger, it was impossible to let go.

Lisa's fear of abandonment had always seemed irrational. She came from a loving family, so when she sensed abandonment, she immediately invalidated her feelings using whatever means necessary to shut them down. She had never associated her "mysterious" feelings with her story, and this made her feel crazy. During her Fourth Step, she connected important pieces of her past—her early abandonment and how she later replayed the past by abandoning herself to sex, alcohol, and other drugs. When she looked at her behavior from the perspective of the injured child, she began to feel compassion for herself. While her feelings were causing her problems in her adult life, they were not an unreasonable consequence of her experience.

She began to put definition on her anger. Her sponsor helped her see the big picture, encouraging her to say what she really wanted to say even though it didn't make sense. She was embarrassed to admit to the feelings she had tried to escape for years. She was angry with her mother for being sick, with the doctor for trying to protect her, with her inner child for being hurt, and with the teenager for trying to get relief.

As she prayed the Seventh Step prayer from the Big Book, the view from her higher self allowed her to see how all the characters in her story were caught in a human dilemma. She felt compassion toward herself and the others in her life.

In the year and a half Lisa has been in recovery, she has developed a healthy reliance on the God of her understanding—a Mother God who will never abandon her. She began dating a few months ago under the careful watch of her sponsor. Her first assignment was to practice breaking up. Her dating agreement includes the following:

1. Informing her potential date up front that she is not looking for a relationship; she's only dating.

2. Avoiding emotional involvement by not dating the same person more than three times.
3. Temporarily abstaining from sex, which she accomplished with the help of Sex and Love Addicts Anonymous (SLAA) meetings.

Lisa is building a storehouse of new experiences. As she heals from her early wound, her confidence grows. She's living in the present and making conscious choices, no longer slipping into the unconscious reactions that characterized her earlier experiences.

Reclaiming Your Power through Ceremony

One way of understanding trauma is that it takes our power and leaves us feeling we are less than we truly are. That feeling of being unlovable or unworthy then shapes the way we relate to everything in life, forming a pattern. The pattern shows up in different attitudes and behaviors in different people. Beneath it all is the loss of our self-worth and our God-given right to make choices. However, self-worth and free choice are part of our spiritual nature. Trauma causes us to lose touch with our spirit but can't destroy it. Symbols and ceremony can unlock the old pattern and reconnect us to spiritual power trapped inside. They work better to heal the heart than words alone.

Creating Sacred Time and Space

You'll need about an hour or two of uninterrupted time. Unplug your phones, turn down the lights, and put on some soft music—if it's not distracting. Silence can be even more powerful. You can do your ceremony alone, with your sponsor, or with a friend. We're suggesting the following items to get you started. After reading this section, you'll know what you want to include in your ceremony.

Gather together a picture of yourself as a child, candles, flowers, rocks or shells, religious symbols, AA anniversary coins, the Big Book, your journal, and any other objects that symbolize to you that something important is about to happen. Include the final results of your Fourth Step, and arrange the items on a coffee table in an attractive and meaningful way.

Option: You might prefer using nature as your sacred space. A small campfire out in the woods or in your back-yard provides a good setting for a ceremony.

Sit quietly for a few minutes and get centered. Begin with a favorite prayer or reading. Light the candles. Take several deep breaths down into your belly to connect with the child within. Reflect on your story while looking at your picture. Go over the list of what you've learned about your-self. Identify the positive skills you've learned and appreci-ate them. Next identify the fears and insecurities you don't want to bring into future relationships.

See your past through the child's eyes, appreciating the struggles you've both been through. Let the child in you realize you've "made it," you're in recovery and getting a whole new chance at life. Be grateful for the child's savvy— *and mean it.* Sit still, breathing. Feel the power building inside as the pattern unlocks. When the time feels right, re-lease it to your Higher Power to be transformed by burning the pages of your Fourth Step. (You can make a safe burning bowl by using a large ashtray or other container filled with sand, or you can take the pages outside.) Look at the flames and smoke and watch as the paper turns to ashes. Fire is an ancient symbol of purification—letting all levels of con-sciousness know the old order is giving way to the new. Set the bowl aside for now and place the child's picture in the center of the altar. Sit quietly and feel your emotions, but be silent.

Ceremony keeps working long after you've blown out the candles. We suggest you let yourself observe the results for a week or more. After your ceremony, you might go for a walk or just be still. Avoid talking too much about your experience. Later you might write your reflections in a journal, but don't reinforce the old pattern by talking or writing about it. You've released it; don't call it back. Think about the "new" happy, joyous, and free you that's being reclaimed.

Transformation: Phoenix on the Rise

The story of the phoenix rising from the fire is a classic tale of transformation. The next part of your ceremony invites your phoenix self to rise from the ashes and reveal a forgotten part of you.

Many people have known from childhood what they wanted to be when they grew up. They carry an image of it in their imagination. When people grow up in healthy families, without years of active addiction, they most likely stay connected to this inner vision and eventually realize it. Some people, however, may be sidetracked by their addiction and worry about having missed some opportunities. But acceptance tells us we are always on time. Our soul guides our destiny: we can't be early or late for it, and nothing can rob us of it. So relax!

Destiny is encoded in our imagination and reveals itself through dreams and visions. For example, in the chapter from the Big Book titled "A Vision for You," it says, "We [the early founders] shall be with you in the Fellowship of the Spirit, and you will surely meet some of us as you trudge the Road of Happy Destiny" (164). This vision tells us we are moving toward happiness, and it lets us know we are not walking alone; we are assisted by the Spirit of all who have gone before us. Many recovering people use this vision as a guiding image in living clean and sober.

YOUR VISION STATEMENT

Organizations use mission statements to guide the decisions of the company, and it works for individuals too. For example, if you have established a vision and then find yourself in a situation that threatens it, your subconscious mind automatically warns you that you are drifting off course. You can learn to recognize this signal. You still have to make a choice, but you'll get a reminder. This is one way of understanding what conscious connection to a Higher Power means.

The following process will connect you with your vision and give you an image to help keep you on course as you venture into the world of clean-and-sober dating. Later, when you move from dating to developing a special relationship with a partner, come back to this exercise and create a vision statement together. It will help guide the relationship.

1. In a sentence or two, describe what you are planning to do.

   I am: (Example: learning how to date clean and sober, staying with my program, continuing to grow and develop spiritually)

2. Identify the feelings that come up for you as you read the statement you just wrote.

   I am feeling: (Example: anxious, frightened, excited, hopeful)

3. Describe what you imagine would be an ideal outcome. Another way of approaching this is to ask yourself what you imagine your Higher Power wants for you as you begin the process of clean-and-sober dating.

> **My ideal outcome:** (Example: I would meet new people, have fun dating, and eventually have a healthy romantic relationship while continuing to develop my spiritual life and grow in my recovery.)

4. Imagine how this will feel when it happens—using positive terms only.

> *Note:* You don't know how it will feel; it hasn't happened yet. You're creating something new for yourself. The point is to *imagine* how it will feel. You want to get into your imagination because that's where the new image comes from. Sometimes you have to list all the negative stuff that's running through your head to get rid of it, but the negatives don't go in your vision statement. You're creating something new and don't want it cast in the old image. The old feelings are bringing the past back; in program talk, you're not letting go.
>
> Completely let go of your fear and imagine having a brand-new experience. What do you imagine it feels like to live without this fear? What does it feel like to succeed in your goal of dating, having fun, having a relationship, and growing spiritually? Remember, if you can imagine it, you can create it.

> **I'd feel:** (Example: grateful, happy, joyous, and free—entitled, like I deserve it)

This was Lisa's "aha" moment. Not feeling deserving was the hidden factor that sabotaged earlier attempts at healthy dating for her. As long as she didn't feel deserving, her choices reflected her low self-esteem. As you go through this process, you will find your hidden factor too.

5. What is a symbolic image of what it feels like to deserve?

> **Image:** (Example: Lisa's symbolic image was a picture of her at the beach, walking in the sunlight. The sand in front of her was washed free of footprints. She felt like she was literally walking into new territory—and deserved to do it.)

Lisa's final step was to ask her Higher Power to remove anything that kept her from feeling deserving so that she could be of greater service.

This process offers a way to gain insight and self-understanding and, ultimately, to have more awareness in making conscious choices. Healing comes in spiritual time, not necessarily according to your clock, as Matt's story shows:

Matt realizes he isn't ready to date yet. He has worked closely with his sponsor for two years. His rage had taken him almost to the point of murder; he entered recovery after a six-month stay in a locked treatment facility.

Matt's father was an active alcoholic, and his drinking binges terrorized the family on a regular basis. Matt's mother would hide him and his brother under the bed while she distracted their father to keep him from attacking them. It usually ended with her getting beaten and Matt and his brother screaming in fright. Matt felt a deep sense of guilt about not being able to protect his mother and brother. He began drinking at twelve years of age to quiet the screams in his head. He quit school and joined the army as soon as he could. His disease progressed, taking him through a series of bad relationships, which always resulted in threatening his girlfriends—as he had learned to do at home. He eventually married, and when he lunged at his wife with a kitchen knife, she called the police and brought charges against him. The army gave him the ultimatum of going into treatment or doing time in the stockade. He took the treatment option.

During his Step work, he saw that his relationships were all tangled up with guilt, fear, and anger—modeled on the one he grew up with. He partnered with women he felt needed "saving." He always became violent, couldn't stop, and psychologically couldn't leave. He felt like the little boy trapped under the bed again.

Matt realized he had learned about relationships from his family as a frightened youngster under the bed. He felt guilty about hiding and for not being able to defend his mother against his father's rage. His pattern of saving women became his way of rescuing her.

Matt is choosing not to date until he has healed from those childhood wounds. He attends meetings regularly and is receiving additional therapy. He's a volunteer at an abused women's shelter, where he works with children. Matt finally found the perfect way to rescue himself, his brother, and his mother and feels it may be exactly what he was born to do.

Summary Points

- Another Fourth Step specifically on past relationships brings new insight.
- Symbol and ceremony help heal past trauma by unlocking your spiritual power and transforming negative patterns.

- Forming a clear vision about your decision to date (as well as anything you are planning to do) helps keep you on course and gives you a warning signal if you start to stray too far off the path. You still have to make a choice about what to do when the "bell" rings.
- Recovery is about making conscious choices. The more we clean out the past, the more self-awareness we bring into the present, and the better the chance of having a new experience.

Healthy relationships depend on each of the two partners being whole people; this means having boundaries. In the next section we'll look at the importance of boundaries in all aspects of your life and as a *must have* for all of your relationships. Boundaries: don't leave home without them.

Chapter Four

Boundaries: We're Not Talking County Line

- Boundaries: the we-shall-intuitively-know part of recovery.
- "No" is a complete sentence; hear it when you say it.
- What hackles, headaches, and shivers all have in common.
- Things your mother didn't tell you.

If you hear the word *boundary* and think county line, study this chapter and consider temporarily putting your dating desire under house arrest. Boundaries encompass basic safety issues as well as likes and dislikes. They are essential to defining who you are and for establishing the rules for how you relate to the world and vice versa. Internal boundaries contain your thoughts, beliefs, and feelings about yourself and about life. They allow you to have your personal version of reality and to coexist with someone who has a different picture without feeling threatened. External boundaries protect your physical space and keep you safe in the world.

"WE SHALL INTUITIVELY KNOW . . ."

Boundaries are natural defenses. Recovery is in part about acting intuitively and depends on respecting your information system. It's up to you to establish your perimeters and your responsibility to maintain the territory. This is known as setting and holding your boundaries; you have to be able to do it whether you're dating or not.

Addiction breaks down your fences. That's pretty much the definition of it—losing control, allowing dangerous things in, going past your limits, not being able to stop even when you want to. Addiction repeatedly put you at risk, getting you to cross the line even when your health and safety were at stake. You may have begun crossing these boundaries as a way of medicating painful emotions, but you ended up distorting your reasoning skills. Then it was no longer a problem for your addiction to keep the supply lines open because you weren't being nagged by your rational mind. Recovery is about reconnecting your natural warning system; it's the we-shall-intuitively-know part of your program.

Boundaries define your side of the me-and-you equation. Where you decide to draw the line is about protecting and controlling *you*, not other people. Boundaries based on preferences—likes and dislikes—are often negotiable, and you can change your mind. In a relationship, for instance, you'll decide how close is too close as you go. Other boundaries about basic safety issues are nonnegotiable.

"No" Is a Complete Sentence

How a person responds to the word *no* tops the list of nonnegotiable boundaries; it's the first test of your ability to hold the line. Upon hearing the word *no*, a healthy person stops immediately. This applies to you too. If you can't hold the line when telling yourself no, you can't hold it with others. If you have clear indications that you're stepping into your old patterns—courting trouble or pushing the edge of good sense—and you decide to push on anyway, you aren't taking care of yourself. You aren't ready for healthy dating—yet.

Likewise, when you say no to someone else and that person continues the behavior, you've met a problem not a potential date. This includes people you know as well as total strangers. You don't have to justify or explain your boundary; going back to the title of this discussion—*"No" is a complete sentence.*

Body Talk and Boundary Setting

Your body is your first line of defense in protecting you from the rest of the world. It gives you physical signals warning you when you're in a potentially dangerous situation—gut feelings. If you aren't in your body and are floating around out there in the ether, it's like flying in bad weather without radar. As you read through this chapter, get a sense of whether your boundary skills are good or if the whole idea is foreign. If you realize you're flying by the seat of your pants, do yourself a favor and think about grounding your plane for now. The world of romance will be there when you're ready. Be honest and loving. It's a cold, hard fact that if you can't love yourself enough to keep yourself safe, no one else will either.

Let's assume you're "in residence" in your body and your alarm system is hooked up. Physical signals warning you of danger are instinctive; they happen at the subconscious level—meaning they occur quicker than your rational mind has time to observe the situation, draw a conclusion, and tell you something's wrong. Instinctive danger signals include body chills, the hair on your neck standing up, goose bumps, stomach cramps, headaches, shuddering, shortness of breath, and going numb. Don't stop with this list. Your body may have other signals; get to know them. A problem occurs when your thinking mind tries to rationalize the warnings away. Conditioning may have taught you to discount the signals, but remember, you can't make the hair on your neck stand up. If it does, something is wrong.

Sensing Boundaries: Feeling Weird

In addition to body cues, emotions also signal potential problems before the thinking mind can comprehend the situation. You might feel yourself emotionally shutting down, feeling angry or resentful, confused, panicky, frustrated, tense or intense, powerless, or defensive without knowing exactly why.

The emotions you're feeling can relate directly to the situation you're in or can be left over from another time, triggered by the present situation. Either way, you need to stop and find out what's going on with you. If you're getting triggered by a lot of different people and circumstances, it's time for an emotional check-in. You might be in danger, or maybe your system is telling you you're not ready for the level of interaction you're attempting. Get safe, listen, and use your rational mind to sort through your experiences, *but don't use it to overrule the emotions you're feeling.* Emotions are messengers. Talk with your sponsor or a trusted friend, and if you're being triggered regularly, consider getting professional counseling.

Remember, chemical dependency and other addictions have messed up your wiring, interfered with your communication system. With time and patience your signals will work again, and with more time and practice you'll learn to listen to them.

Warning: Danger Ahead!

Certain boundaries are expected in society. If a person (including you) is lacking them, it could indicate mental or emotional problems that are more than you can handle without professional help. Here's a list of questions to help identify abusive tendencies or potentially dangerous behaviors that indicate trouble:

- Am I able to hold the line—hearing and heeding my own no?
- Is the other person respecting my no?
- Am I feeling abused?
- Is there explosive behavior or the silent treatment?
- Am I blaming myself or feeling blamed?
- Am I being overly critical or feeling criticized?
- Does it seem like I always have to give in or adapt?
- Am I feeling crazy—doubting my perceptions?
- Am I comfortable about how decisions are made, or are there constant attempts to control?
- Is there any name-calling, anger, sarcasm, ridicule, or shaming?
- Are there spoken or implied threats or ultimatums of any kind such as "I'll leave if . . ." or "I'll tell if . . ."
- Am I feeling cut off from friends, or am I cutting myself off from friends?
- Do I feel dangerously isolated or crowded?
- Do I find myself going over and over the same requests?
- Does it seem like options are decreasing—like my life is getting smaller?

Be Discriminating

Boundaries range from basic human rights to personal likes and dislikes. Some boundaries only reveal themselves as you go and change with time and with the right person. You're wise to know two important facts about boundaries. First, you need to know your boundaries and be completely in control of when and with whom you allow changes.

Second, assessing someone's boundaries isn't taking that person's inventory; it's *your* responsibility to yourself to be able to make an honest appraisal of someone's behavior and decide what level of interaction is safe for you.

Following are five classifications of boundaries, including common characteristics to look for in each category. Use this list as a starting point, adding your own characteristics as you see fit.

Physical Boundaries

Physical boundaries include knowing when you are or another is

- standing or sitting too close
- touching without permission
- being too loud, talking too much, not talking enough
- acting sexually inappropriate (for example, sexual comments, unwelcome physical advances, suggestive invitations)
- participating in sex unwillingly
- unable to maintain basic healthy habits, including diet, sleep, exercise, and cleanliness
- driving dangerously or disregarding basic safety
- financially irresponsible (for example, no job, not living within means, not paying bills)

Emotional Boundaries

Emotional boundaries include knowing when you are or another is

- sharing inappropriately, that is, disclosing too much too fast or withholding information
- angry (a lot of the time)

- cursing excessively
- not taking responsibility for personal emotional needs or behaviors (for example, "You make me feel . . ." or "You made me do it.")
- manufacturing problems to be "helped" or "saved"
- people pleasing
- controlling you or others outside the relationship
- mistaking kindness for love
- falling in love too easily
- shutting down emotionally
- being unkind to self or others
- lacking a full range of emotions
- lacking friends or is not a member of a regular group (for example, home group, church, or other social setting)

Mental Boundaries

Mental boundaries include knowing when you are or another is

- having opinions rather than relying solely on others' interpretation of reality
- able to reason and form another opinion when appropriate
- able to discuss differences without feeling threatened
- being confused, confusing, or spacey
- having obsessive-compulsive thoughts
- willing to take personal responsibility for actions
- able to assess a problem and meet it with a solution

Spiritual Boundaries

Spiritual boundaries include knowing when you are or another is

- honest (no lying, cheating, or stealing)
- trustworthy (keeps agreements, shows up on time, and follows through on promised actions)
- acting with integrity, that is, behaving consistently with stated values
- being respectful toward self and others
- exhibiting a lightness of being, that is, approaching life confidently and with a sense of humor and creativity

Boundaries around Addiction

Boundaries around addiction include knowing when you are or another is

- working a program, if addicted
- able to drink responsibly, if not addicted
- having a problem if a date indulges socially and, if so, whether it can be worked out
- using illegal drugs ("legal" is a boundary!)
- showing signs of emotional, physical, or mental abuse
- showing signs of self-abuse (emotional, physical, or mental)

Before the Horse Leaves the Barn

Like the old saying about the futility of locking the barn after the horse leaves, boundary discernment needs to happen *before* you get emotionally involved. Once the emotions are revved up, your thinking begins playing tricks on you—like convincing you that it's not as bad as you think and that you've been too hasty in setting up all these rules. You begin to rationalize that you're not really feeling what you're feeling or that your feelings aren't important.

The truth is, all relationships have their ups and downs, and the line between compassion and foolhardiness can be a fine one. While feelings are real, as in they are *really* happening inside of you, sometimes the conclusions you draw based solely on emotions aren't true; they don't match the situation. Even so, sometimes they are the only thing standing between you and a very dangerous situation. When emotions are sending you signals, it's important to figure out what's going on before you get too immersed in the situation in order to have the safest response.

Anyone can get lured or tricked into a relationship with an abusive person. They're potential predators and look for ways around your defenses. They watch for openings. Whether they know what they're doing or not isn't the point. You need to recognize when you feel you're not being treated right, investigate your feeling further, and take appropriate action. If you find you are justifying away another's behavior or yours, you are in a red-flag situation.

Things You May Not Know

If you are the survivor of physical or sexual abuse, your sense of boundaries has been tampered with; your alarm system has been turned off through no fault of your own. This jeopardizes your basic survival skills in all areas of life. If you haven't gotten therapy for your abuse, or if it didn't specifically include boundary work, you might want to seek further healing before entering the dating scene.

Sex abuse survivors have particular trouble with sexual boundaries. Part of their behavior pattern includes getting into sexual relations easily, without planning or forethought—an unsafe practice itself and usually involving unsafe partners. Without healing, victims are likely to go from relationship to relationship, not really wanting sex but having it because of previous conditioning and not being able to say no. Most survivors say these encounters are not pleasurable; they endure them through dissociation.

In particular, early abuse disarms the natural warning system. It leaves victims unable to perceive danger, and even when danger becomes obvious, they are unlikely to respond to it in a self-protective way. While assault is never the fault of the victim, sexual abuse survivors often inadvertently put themselves in dangerous situations at dangerous times. In an ideal world they would be safe sitting on a bench dressed in a tank top and short shorts waiting for the midnight bus, but that isn't life on life's terms.

THINGS YOUR MOTHER NEVER TOLD YOU

Dating is meant to be fun, and you're supposed to be able to relax and have a good time. The likelihood that you'll enjoy yourself increases proportionately with your ability to set and maintain good boundaries. Being armed with good information is critical to the process. Knowing the dangers involved in dating is the best insurance for having a good time and returning home to talk about it. You've heard the old saying "forewarned is forearmed"; a walk through some worst-case scenarios will help make the ideal situation more possible.

Date Rape Is a Reality

A high percentage of rapes happen between two people who know one another. Many of these happen on a first date or by a former romantic acquaintance. Whether it's called date rape or acquaintance rape, any advance after the word *no* is rape.

The definition of rape is the crime of being forced to have sex against your will. Just what constitutes rape, however, is riddled with complications. Stereotypes still abound, reinforcing that it's the man's job to initiate sex and aggression is just part of the "game." Many still believe it's the woman's job to play "hard to get" and that nothing happens if she doesn't want it to happen.

We now know that rape isn't about the aggressor being overcome with sexual passion; it's about using sex as power. The shortest and most direct definition of rape bears repeating: *rape is any advance after the word* no.

Fact and Fiction about Date Rape

Here is some useful information from the South Eastern Centre Against Sexual Assault (www.secasa.com.au) and the National Center for Victims of Crime (www.ncvc.org) for men and women about date rape:

- Fiction: Rape is a crime committed by strangers.
- Fact: Every minute, 1.3 women are forcibly raped, and in three-quarters of the cases, they know the assailant.

- Fiction: Rape is a crime committed against women.
- Fact: As many as 43 percent of males reported being the victim of violence from dating partners at least once. Assailants can be women or other men.

- Fiction: Date rape only happens when two people don't know each other very well.
- Fact: It isn't uncommon to be raped by someone you've known for a long time; former lovers and even spouses rape.

Men: Women can and do give mixed messages, and you may fall prey to enticement. To protect yourself from becoming the victim of a confusing situation, you might find the following suggestions helpful:

- Regardless of what has been going on, when she says no, she means do not continue.
- Women aren't necessarily "asking for it" by the way they dress.
- Being alone with you in a private place doesn't mean she is saying yes to sex.
- Women accept touching, holding, and kissing as an end in itself; it isn't necessarily foreplay.
- If you haven't talked the whole thing out before the passion heats up, don't let the moment carry you away.
- A woman can be intimidated by your strength. Her ability to struggle may seem weak or insincere, "not all that real," but believe it.

Women: Men use different sexual signaling than women do. Kissing, hugging, and touching can be interpreted as permission for intercourse, so can the way you dress, choices about being alone, and suggestive remarks. To help prevent becoming the victim of a sexual crime, keep the following guidelines in mind:

- Be clear. Don't play the teasing game. Being suggestive one minute and not the next leads to confusion.
- Don't go to his apartment for an intimate evening and be surprised if he makes advances.
- Touching or rubbing against a man's penis, even through clothing, is going to start something he'll want to finish.

Date-Rape Drugs

Something else that can make you vulnerable to date rape is the use of date-rape drugs. The term *date-rape drug* usually applies to the following drugs:

- Rohypnol, known on the street as roofies or roaches
- Gamma hydroxybutyrate (GHB), also known as Liquid G, G, Georgia Home Boy, and Easy Lay
- Ketamine hydrochloride, also known as K, Vitamin K, and Special K
- Ecstasy (MDMA), called Adam, Bean, E, M, and Roll

The widespread availability of these drugs has put a very powerful weapon in the hands of sexual predators. These drugs are almost impossible to detect; they are tasteless, odorless, and colorless. All traces will leave the body within seventy-two hours of ingestion and are not found in routine toxicology screens or blood tests. Date-rape drugs are easily slipped into both alcoholic and nonalcoholic drinks or food and are fast acting.

GHB produces alcohol-like effects and can be felt within fifteen minutes. It can cause headaches, shaking, seizures, drowsiness, nausea, irregular heartbeat, and vomiting. When mixed with alcohol, it can cause loss of consciousness and possibly death.

The effects of **Rohypnol** begin within thirty minutes and may last for eight hours or more. They include memory impairment, amnesia, drowsiness, visual disturbances, dizziness, impaired motor skills and judgment, slurred speech, confusion, gastrointestinal disturbances, and urinary retention.

Ketamine can cause a person to feel "separated" from

her body; bring on amnesia, hallucinations, and numbness; and dangerously lower the heart rate leading to oxygen starvation in the brain and muscles. It can also produce temporary paralysis.

Ecstasy can cause mental confusion, depression, sleep problems, drug cravings, anxiety, and paranoia for weeks after ingesting. Physical symptoms often include muscle tension, involuntary teeth clenching, nausea, blurred vision, rapid eye movement, faintness, and chills or sweating.

You can reduce the risk of accidentally ingesting a date-rape drug by following these suggestions:

1. Don't accept open drinks (alcoholic or non-alcoholic) from people you don't know or don't trust; this includes all drinks that come in a glass.
2. If you are at a bar or club, always get your drink directly from the bartender, and do not take your eyes off the bartender or your order; don't use the waiter or let an acquaintance or stranger go to the bar for you.
3. Only accept drinks in closed containers at parties.
4. Never leave your drink unattended or turn your back on your table.
5. Do not drink from open beverage sources such as punch bowls, pitchers, or tubs.
6. Keep your eyes and ears open; if there is talk of date-rape drugs, usually called by their street names, or you notice anything suspicious such as friends seeming too intoxicated for the amount they've had to drink, do what you can to help by alerting them and helping them to leave. Regardless, you should leave the party or club and call the police.

Innuendos Looking for a Place to Land

Another signal to be alert to is sexual innuendos. If you don't want sex, a wrestling match, or to be accused of teasing, watch out for the following invitations or situations:

- "Why don't you relax and let me give you a back rub (including shoulder and feet massages and toe sucking)?"
- "Can you help me with this zipper?"
- "Would you mind coming in for just a minute while I check the house for burglars?"
- "Let's just stretch out on the bed and cuddle. I promise nothing will happen until you're ready."
- Late night walks on a deserted beach (particularly when carrying a blanket).
- Naked hot-tubbing or skinny-dipping.

Almost all date rapes include alcohol or other drugs. Because you are most likely in recovery (or dating someone in recovery), the assumption is you won't be engaging in that behavior. If, however, being with someone who is drinking is a problem for you and if not drinking becomes a problem for your date, it's a sign to move on.

Stalking: Not a Time to Be Polite

Nobody likes to hear that the relationship isn't working or, worse, that it's over. It is normal for the person being left to resist and need to talk further. Have such talks in a public place and be very direct about what you're saying. Be absolutely clear in setting your boundary, letting the person know there is no possibility of having any kind of relationship—ever. Don't try to be nice by saying it's over for now or maybe we can talk again later. If someone persists in attempting to make contact with you after you have terminated a relationship and clearly stated that you do not want further contact, this could be considered stalking. A stalker has an obsession with you, distorting or hearing only what he wants to hear. Any openings in your behavior or communication will be interpreted as an invitation. If this person continues to overstep your boundary, report the incidents to the police for evaluation.

There aren't absolute ways to know what is stalking versus breaking-up behavior. Use common sense, and if things feel weird, a call to the police or rape crisis center can help you evaluate your situation. Rape crisis centers usually allow you to ask questions anonymously.

Caution! Boundary Alarms

Not all boundary alarms indicate a dangerous problem, but all are indications of potential trouble. Proceed with caution if you encounter any of the following situations:

- A person who needs to be told "no" more than once. Is it a hearing problem or a problem hearing?
- A person who spends a lot of time trying to change your mind. This applies to anything from eating broccoli to having sex.
- A person who has a problem changing a meeting time or place, even if you've done your best to give good notice.
- A person who constantly reshuffles the rules or plans or has an absolute inability to make any changes.
- A person who doesn't respect a boundary you set when she doesn't think it's important. (For example, "I don't see why you need to . . .")

It's a cold, cruel world out there, and at the same time, it's a wonderful, friendly place. Having good boundaries and knowing what to watch for makes the second part of that statement more likely to be your experience. As was mentioned earlier, some boundaries are negotiated as you go; they're an ongoing part of putting the *consciousness* in the *conscious choices* you make about dating, relating, and mating.

SUMMARY POINTS

- Good boundaries are indications of good self-awareness; they begin at home with setting your rules and going by them.
- Establish your boundaries and practice holding them *before* getting into a dating relationship. Dating tests your ability to keep them.
- Dating is the time to assess your date's boundaries *before* getting emotionally involved. This is not "taking someone's inventory"; it is self-protection.
- Safe and happy dating depends on self-love and the willingness to keep yourself safe, on self-knowledge, and on knowledge of the potential dangers you might encounter.

Next you'll have the opportunity to meet your committee—the sometimes annoying characters who live in your head. Once you sort through the voices, you'll find they can become your very own support system.

Chapter Five *

Meet the Committee

- The cantankerous characters in your head can become your best friends.
- Finally, the instruction book.
- Miranda's rebel has a night on the town.
- Jesse thanks God and Greyhound.
- Your lover and warrior: good safe sex!

The committee is that inharmonious horde of "whoever" that hammers away in your head 24-7. These committee members want you to think they have your best interest at heart, but they don't always. What does yours like to say? "You're not good enough or smart enough?" "You should be more like your brother?" How about, "Go ahead, take the biggest piece of cake, fatso!"

Recovery is about getting to know what's going on inside of you. However, stepping into your inner world and running smack into a toxic committee is enough to throw even Dr. Phil into a codependent tailspin. It's no wonder you'd rather spend time in someone else's head than your own. Hopefully, by now you have put some faces on these voices and realize they don't belong to you. They're echoes of the past, such as Aunt Minnie from Pittsburgh who thought you weren't quite pretty enough—not like your sister. Or your Uncle Bob from Birmingham who smelled like bourbon, squeezed your hand till you dropped to your knees, and then told you, "Big boys don't cry."

Taking Back the Castle

Once you get these toxic characters out of your head, your own world opens up and you find the real version of "yours truly." You'll discover talents you didn't know existed. These characters, known as archetypes, represent human qualities we all hold in common—such as love, creativity, curiosity, nurturing, bravery, a sense of adventure, love of freedom, need for emotional connection, and a sense of the sacred—but with our own personal spin. (These archetypes have the potential to become toxic when just a select few dominate our psyche.)

Recovering people often say that other folks seem to have an instruction book that they didn't get. This is just another way that our lack of emotional maturity tricks us. We may look like grown-ups but have the feelings and skills of kids a lot of the time. But there is good news: archetypes carry the instructions for basic abilities, or life skills.

When we first arrive in recovery, we're only drawing from a few of the dozen or so archetypes available, usually the rebel, a wounded child, and a version of our toxic parents (or perhaps Aunt Minnie and Uncle Bob). Maturity is a process of becoming aware of our vulnerabilities as well as our strengths and abilities. Archetypes are a helpful way of identifying our different facets and will eventually bring greater insight.

Archetypes awaken as your natural developmental process reactivates in recovery. Spending time with a sponsor as well as going to meetings where you hear different viewpoints help you realize there is a variety of ways to look at any one topic. The ability to see things from different perspectives gives you depth; it's a characteristic of a fully developed person. Life isn't black and white.

WAKING UP TO MORE OPTIONS

Archetypes are impulses in the psyche and show up as characters. Each has the innate intelligence (common sense) that goes with a particular human task or responsibility. Each has its own attitude, beliefs, and behaviors that you come to recognize. Often in early recovery you don't have enough self-awareness to know when one of your characters takes over. When that happens, you are seeing the world through one perspective only, missing the full range of options.

As was mentioned earlier, there are often a dozen or so main archetypes. We're going to simplify and identify only eight characters to represent a typical assortment you might meet in your inner world. (Keep in mind that archetypes aren't gender specific; the use of male or female pronouns is for demonstration purposes only.) Those in dark type in the following diagram are the three that are usually dominant in early sobriety. The others will eventually wake up—or sober up. When the archetypes enter your awareness, you'll get a more balanced picture of the world and have access to many more skills needed to negotiate life on life's terms.

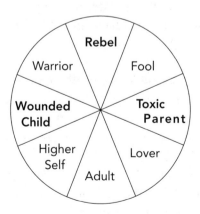

The Rebel, the Toxic Parent, and the Wounded Child

Rebel with a Cause

The rebel part of you appears confident. He acts cocky, laughs at authority, and goes out if the way to break the rules. "Skate fast, die young" is his motto. The rebel doesn't take instruction well (of course not, he knows everything). In actuality, the rebel is often a hurting child in a grown-up body. He shoots from the hip. His perceived mission is to fight against external authority, which keeps him focused outside of himself, disconnected from his own spirit. He's like an animal sensing danger and puffing himself up to scare away the enemy but hurting himself more than those he wants to hurt. He runs the show on adrenaline, a product of his constant fear, medicating himself with addictive living.

As you will see, when the rebel is healed, he is an important part of your psyche; he's your free spirit. It becomes a problem, however, when this part of your psyche (or any of the other parts) takes over. The goal is to get all parts working together. When each part understands its job and knows others are doing theirs, your inner life runs smoother. The rebel is then really free to "do his thing." The freer he becomes, the less rebellious he is and the less likely you both are to end up in the ditch.

Everybody Loves Raymond's Mother

When the toxic parent is in charge of your inner world, the tendency is to try and control everything and everyone. She has the natural urge to take care of people, but her efforts come off as bossy. She "saves" people by telling them what to do. She's a finger wagger—judging and criticizing—and says "it's for your own good." She can also get abusive, doling out love or withholding it to make her point. Her chronic "fixing" of others while neglecting her own needs leaves her in a lot of pain—which she medicates with addiction. If she would only get some boundaries and stay home and take care of you rather than everyone else, things would settle down inside.

Grandmother, What Big Teeth You Have

The wounded child is the result of growing up in a home where toxic parenting was the way of life. The child has been abused, neglected, and has often had to take charge of the family because of the immaturity of the parents. The child arrives in adult life overburdened and overwhelmed by taking on adult responsibility. She is way too open and trusting, unable to tell the wolf from Grandma. Other times she is hypervigilant, unable to let go; she trusts no one and doesn't know how to relax or play. The wounded child lives in fear, isolation, loneliness, and abandonment—using addiction to manage the pain. As the child heals, she becomes playful, imaginative, and creative. The child doesn't "grow up" but remains a part of you that is innocent and childlike—free of adult responsibilities. This part of your psyche is the core of your creativity.

———————

Think about it! Would you trust any of these three characters to go out for ice cream, let alone to find a date for Saturday night? Your rebel heads straight for the biker bar—the one with the "trouble" sign over the door. Your toxic parent craves problems to fix and hooks you up with someone who has an endless supply. Your wounded child really shouldn't be out alone after dark; she's apt to go home with anyone who offers her a ride.

———————

A Rebel's Night Out

Miranda's story shows how all three of these wounded characters took turns in her head, swaying her judgment and manipulating her choices.

Miranda's been clean and sober for three weeks, and she's edgy. The moon is full over the parking lot of the clubhouse as she heads to her regular meeting. Suddenly she is seized with resentment; she feels cheated, ripped off by her circumstances. *Haven't I done everything they told me to do?* she asks herself. *Nothing ever works* is her quick reply, followed even more rapidly by *F—k it!* Just then she notices the silhouette of a man in the shadows outside the back door. He motions her toward him with a nod. Miranda glances at his body art and asks him if he's new in town. Within a very short period of time—about four and a half minutes—they leave together in Miranda's car.

The stranger swerves recklessly through traffic. Miranda is only slightly aware that her stomach is tying itself in knots. He runs a red light nearly causing a three-car pileup. She thinks she remembers him shouting an obscenity at a distraught driver. Miranda's ears are ringing, her breath is shallow, and she is going numb from the neck down. They park near the river, and the stranger begins groping her roughly. She asks him to quit. He laughs, saying, "Right, baby, you came out here with me to look at the moon."

They have sex. Miranda begs him to use a condom; he refuses. Afterward he drives downtown and gets out of the car near a strip club. "See ya around," he mutters, not looking her in the eyes. On the way home, Miranda's memory of the evening begins to reshape itself. By the time she gets to her house, it seemed like they'd had a great time.

It's not difficult to see where Miranda's rebel took over,

convincing her she was due a little excitement. Hadn't she done everything they'd been telling her? Once in control, her rebel immediately craved adrenaline, and the stranger looked like he could supply it. The gut-wrenching ride across town felt like the danger she grew up with, and it triggered the wounded child in her. She was spinning out of control, disconnecting, like she had done to protect herself in the past. By the time they got to the river, she was no longer in her body. In a confusing way, the child had taken cover and taken charge at the same time. She abandoned herself much the way her toxic parents had always abandoned her when she needed them to be strong. On the way home, her child began retelling the story in a magical way that she could deal with—smoothing out the rough edges, skipping the sordid details.

Recovery is about healing these characters and developing other parts of yourself to bring balance, support, and the skills needed for a rich, full life. The rebel isn't quite so frisky when he isn't pumped up on crystal meth. He eventually becomes teachable, mainly because the program doesn't impose rules but offers suggestions (it seems you never outgrow your love of freedom). You learn good parenting through sponsorship and through the hope, strength, and experience of others. You eventually learn how to take care of yourself and keep the child safe. As the child heals, you find you are laughing and having fun again, more than you thought was possible.

MEETING THE REST OF THE "FAMILY"

Following are some of the characters you'll eventually find in your inner world. They usually appear first in their toxic state as shown in the first column. The second column shows how they function later with some recovery under their belts. How many do you recognize?

Injured Rebel	Recovered Rebel
Defiant	Seeks justice
Hates all authority	Fights false authority
Seeks dangerous behavior	Seeks adventure
Pushes the edge	Explores new horizons
Denies fear	Finds inner strength
Fights with everything	Feels free at last!

Wounded Child	Recovered Child
Feels guilty	Realizes innocence
Is naive	Learns whom to trust
Worries	Is playful
Shuts down	Is creative
Disconnects	Is intuitive
Feels numb	Is sensuous

Toxic Inner Parent	Recovered Inner Parent
Controlling	Protective
Smothering	Nurturing
Abusive	Caring
Shaming	Encouraging
Neglectful	Pays attention
Needy and immature	Confident and wise

Toxic Adult	Recovered Adult
Greedy or squandering	Good financial skills
Antagonistic	Forms friendships
Too rigid or wishy-washy	Flexible and able to mediate
Irresponsible	Responsible
Muddled values	Possesses clarity and integrity
Inauthentic	Self-actualized

Lethal Lover

Violates
Disheartened
Taker, uses others
Acts sexy
Manipulative
Destroys

Recovered Lover

Appreciates
Romantic
Generous
Is passionate and caring
Open and honest
Creates

Toxic Warrior

Invades others' space
Takes advantage
Is self-serving
Commitment: yeah, right!
Jaded and cynical
Creates chaos

Recovered Warrior

Protects your boundary
Defends your honor
Serves others
Loyal and steadfast
Idealistic
Keeps order

Toxic Fool

Duped, misled
Magical thinking
Acts foolishly
Lacks skills
Behaves oddly
Silly

Recovered Fool

Spiritual seeker
Recognizes mystery and faith
Uses discernment
Is willing to learn
Finds true uniqueness
Humorous

Higher Self (Can't Be Toxic)

Has a spiritual center
Brings wisdom
Sees big picture
Is altruistic
Has a God-self connection
Loves

Transforming Your Inner World

In the transformed inner world, the committee becomes your "dream team." For example, the healed inner parent learns how to care for the inner child and to make healthy choices. The child is free of responsibility and learns to relax, laugh, and play again; your creativity awakens. The toxic fool is the part of us that has always been searching for God. Foolishly, she sought transcendence through addiction; in recovery she finally finds her Higher Power. You've heard people say, "You'd have to be a fool to believe that." It's through the fool that we find God.

The rebel and adult bring balance to each other. The rebel keeps the adult from getting too "invested" in the business world, reminding him that we make it all up anyway. The only real things are the wind in your face and the roaring Harley between your legs. The inner adult appreciates the rebel's irrepressible spirit but keeps him from dangerous behavior by strapping on a helmet.

Key Players in the Game of Love

The lover and the warrior are your key players when it comes time for dating and relating. They may seem like an unlikely pair, yet when they are mated in your psyche, they are the perfect combination of beauty and order, passion and reason, vulnerability and boundaries. Again, archetypes aren't gender specific, but the lover represents the feminine part of the psyche, and the warrior is your inner male.

Lover of Beauty

The lover holds your higher values; she's the part of you that seeks love and beauty. She can find them in the arts or a relationship—ideally both. She is captured by music, poetry, and romance.

Without the balance of the warrior, the lover lacks common sense. She's hopelessly romantic and can easily fall victim to her boundless passion. She brings home all sorts of strays—cats, dogs, and people. The lover isn't concerned with mundane matters like fleas, disease, or anything that isn't "lovely." She can't imagine commitment or sticking with someone when the going gets tough. She hates haggling. It's just "lovelier" to find someone new.

If the lover in your psyche takes over without the warrior, she can be needy and demanding—convincing you that finding a partner is a matter of life and death. She'll make you believe you're nothing without love.

Warrior: Our Knight in Shining Armor

The warrior in our psyche watches over and protects our lover. He creates safety and keeps order by guarding our boundaries; he holds the line. He is skilled at diplomacy and preventing war. His loyalty is beyond question. He upholds the lover's values, defends her honor, and brings the element of steadfastness and commitment to relationships. He is the knight in shining armor.

The warrior's prowess and fierce dedication free the lover in you to do what she does best—love. He sets the stage for romance, arranging the flowers, lighting the candles, and hiring the violinists. He makes sure you don't squander your love on someone who is unworthy of you. He respects boundaries and would never use his strength against anyone or allow anyone else to use it against you. In return, the lover falls completely and deeply in love with her own inner male. Together they are the perfect combination of beauty and order.

Without the lover, the warrior can become brutal and

self-destructive. He pillages rather than protects—taking what he wants in the way of sex with no sense of responsibility or commitment. He can become jealous and overbearing, be too protective, and build a fortress around you; you can't get out, and no one can get near you.

THE PERFECT COUPLE

When the lover and warrior meet in the psyche, the combination is both powerful and sexy. Under the protection of the warrior, the lover can let down her defenses and love fully and passionately. If you are this lover's lucky partner, she might astonish you with a surprise visit—a spontaneous and passionate interlude. Clearing the desk with a sweep of her arm, she'll entice you into sex. Her warrior will make sure it's *your* office, the sex is *"safe,"* and the door is *locked!*

When the lover and warrior join forces, you feel loved and loving and willing to wait for the right time and an appropriate partner—one who reflects your high self-esteem and who will treat you as well as you have learned to treat yourself. Courtship will be romantic and ongoing, whether you're with another or courting yourself. Tender and strong, the inner warrior brings out your softer side—your femininity. Flowers and music will be a regular feature of your relationship, and when the lover and warrior marry within your own psyche, you will enjoy an evening at home listening to your favorite music by candlelight alone or with someone else.

Notice that there are only two archetypes directly involved in finding and maintaining your relationship; the rest of the gang continues to be active in all the other aspects of your life—work, school, meetings, friendships, sports, health, hobbies, and so on. You may mistakenly think you can get everything you need from one person or are the one who tries to be all things to another. No relationship can fulfill your every need. Becoming acquainted with archetypes is one way to get perspective and proportion on expectations and to keep from going overboard in any area of your life. Of course, some of the characters may need to attend appropriate Twelve Step meetings to be all they can be.

MISERY MATCH: JESSE MEETS MIRANDA

You remember Miranda and her moonstruck misadventure. Let's take a look at what happens when Jesse meets Miranda before his warrior has surfaced to protect his overzealous inner lover. Jesse has a year in recovery and feels older and wiser than Miranda—which, in Jesse's inner world, translates into being responsible for her. Oh, Jesse, if you'd only waited.

Jesse is the oldest of four kids. His mother was an alcoholic, and his father was a "traveling" man. He remembers seeing his father only a couple of times when he came through town; they weren't good memories. Jesse became the man of the family when he was six years old, helping his brothers and sister get through school, delaying his own education in the process. Later, when he went to college, he began experimenting with drugs but couldn't stop. He dropped out of school and got a job driving a truck until drug screening caught up with him. He struggled with a variety of jobs, working whenever he could.

Although he could barely keep food on his table, he often brought others home who were down on their luck. The last one hit him over the head with a tire iron for the thirteen dollars he had in his pocket, leaving him for dead. Jesse found his way into recovery, where he eventually met Miranda. He recalls how she had a lost kitten look in her eyes (it was two days after her encounter with the stranger), and he just wanted to bring her home and take care of her.

He fixed dinner as she sat on the couch paging through a magazine. She could hardly eat because of all her worries; she was three days late with the rent and broke. Jesse reached into his pocket and handed her the money. She looked at him in wonderment. He remembers that as the moment he fell in love with her.

He courted Miranda in as much style as his credit cards could "afford." He bought flowers, took her out to dinner, and showered her with affection. Miranda accepted his gifts but felt smothered. Secretly, she longed for the stranger in the parking lot. Without a regular supply of adrenaline, she was getting depressed. Jesse just knew he could cheer her up, and on her birthday he surprised her with an engagement ring. Miranda's eyes betrayed her, and Jesse had a sinking feeling. When he left the room for a moment, she walked out of the apartment and caught the westbound Greyhound for Montana. Jesse was stunned. He took the empty ring box down to the corner pub and began drinking that night.

Jesse's experience with Miranda could have turned out differently with help from a few of his archetypes. To begin with, his wounded child was running the show; he needed time out to heal before dating. His lover was all tangled up with his toxic parent; without boundaries he couldn't keep them straight. His warrior was AWOL and didn't have a clue.

Meet Your Committee

Naming your archetypal characters and having regular conversations with them helps wake them up. After a while you can tell who's influencing you. For example, if you get antsy on the job, you'll be able to know whether it's your rebel telling you to "take this job and shove it" or your higher self letting you know you could do better. Many times when you're feeling sad and lonely, you may think you need somebody to love you when it's really your own inner child that wants you to take better care of yourself.

Remember, all your characters want to be helpful, but they've picked up some strange ideas and odd habits along the way. It takes a little finesse on your part to recognize their hidden gifts and bring out their best. They're all a part of you, but you are the decision maker. They're your "dream team," but you're the dreamer. They work for you, and you pay the bill.

Here's a list of common archetypes to get you started in meeting your own. Choose a character from the list or find one in your inner world and see how "it" answers the questions that follow.

Accountant	Fool	Rescuer
Adult	Healer	Ruler
Adventurer	Higher Self	Savior
Artist	Judge	Spiritual Seeker
Caregiver	Lover	Student
Child	Martyr	Teacher
Critic	Parent	Warrior
Explorer	Rebel	Wise One
Others:		

Character Questions

1. What is this character's name?

2. What would his bumper sticker say?

3. What is her favorite song?

4. How does this character dress?

5. What's her job in your inner world?

6. Does he need anything from you to make his job easier?

7. Is she out of balance—taking over or not being strong enough?

8. What character would this one team up with for balance?

9. How can this character best be of service?

10. What jobs would this character absolutely *not* be good at? (For example, your inner child or your rebel can't take care of the checkbook or be relied on to select a date.)

Following are different ways people have identified their inner characters. You can pretty well guess who's who by their names.

The Hobo	Motorcycle Mama	Big Daddy
Bag Lady	Bad Boy	Violet
Earth Mother	John Wayne	The Vamp
Scrooge	Madonna	Lover Boy
Busy Bee	Amazon Woman	Tarzan

Meeting the various parts of yourself and getting their perspective leads to a full and balanced life. It makes you an interesting person—creative and fun. It makes life richer and more exciting as you are more likely to try your hand at new things. It takes a little time but is worth the effort. When you know who you are and gain mastery over basic life skills, it's like finally getting the instruction book. (Look at exercise 1 in appendix A, "Balancing Your Medicine Wheel," for more on archetypes.)

Summary Points

- You arrive in recovery with only a fraction of your full potential developed. It's a time for maturing emotionally, discovering more about yourself, and learning how the world works—not a time to make life choices.
- Archetypes are characters in the psyche that represent various skills and talents. Out of the dozen or so, only two are directly involved in dating; the rest of them stay focused on other parts of your life.
- Your lover and warrior take an effective team approach to finding an appropriate date—combining passion and reason. Others, such as the parent, child, or rebel don't need to be dating.
- As you meet and greet these characters, you learn more about yourself and develop life skills and talents. The fully developed person has access to all the archetypes.

Let's say you've honed all the skills suggested here—cleaned house, established your boundaries, befriended your inner world, and now you're ready to begin the next phase of Easy Does It dating. The questions are "Where to go?" and "What to do?" The next chapter has lots of suggestions on places to go to meet new people and lots of ideas for things to do on a clean-and-sober date.

Chapter Six *

Into Action: Where to Go and What to Do

- Pros and cons of program relationships
- Ideas for expanding your world
- Clean and sober and asking for a date
- First date: where to go and what to expect

The big question facing almost everyone at this point is where to meet people now that you aren't making the rounds of the local pubs. This can be as challenging to non-addicted singles as it is to you. In this chapter, you'll find an extensive list of places to go and activities to investigate that will support your interests as well as broaden your social horizons. First, let's cover a few suggested ground rules for where *not* to go looking for potential dates.

Our Suggested Off Limits

Cruising Meetings

This is too much like dropping a hook into the goldfish bowl. Not fair game. Meetings are about recovering from a life-threatening disease. It's sacred space. You're there to carry the recovery message—not a message about meeting later. At the same time, it's almost impossible to go to meetings and never have the idea of dating someone pop into your head. You form intimate spiritual bonds within the fellowship, which is seductive. But you need to be able to be vulnerable and not be taken advantage of; you need to trust others in the group. It's likely that you may meet someone in recovery who fits your bill almost exactly, and many good relationships have grown out of shared recovery. However, you shouldn't *cruise* meetings with the intention of scouting a date. The topic of recovering couples is further discussed in Chapter 9: Variations on a Theme.

Surfing the Net

Today, online matchmaking is the most popular dating venue, even surpassing sports bars as a place to meet. It's surely convenient in our busy world where lack of community and shortage of time are factors in many lives. Success stories of couples who meet online are growing—a folk legend in the making. The intent is not to knock online dating; however, it doesn't fit the process being presented here. Personal ads and online dating services are goal-oriented rather than process-oriented. The dating process promoted here seeks to expand your world, and Internet dating seems to shrink it. Sitting alone in your room reading descriptions that may not have anything to do with a living person is isolating. All too soon you find yourself searching files to "find" someone. Your dating plan calls for meeting new people, honing your social skills, and exploring new activities.

In addition, the anonymity of the online environment can provide a false sense of protection, encouraging potentially harmful risk taking. Often people write things they probably wouldn't say to a "real" person. This type of environment seems to play easily with the addictive psyche. Even non-addicted people can find they are suddenly obsessed—constantly checking their e-mail, searching listings, feeling hurt when someone doesn't e-mail back (taking something personally that isn't the least bit personal).

If, after considering all this, you decide to explore dating through the Internet anyway, you'll find this guide will still work for you.

Old Playgrounds

You've no doubt heard the suggestion about changing playmates and playpens. Going back into bars is too much like climbing back into the old playpen. Bars can trigger your addiction, and they are noisy; you can't really get to know a person in that setting. It increases the odds of acting on a spur of the moment encounter rather than using a careful assessment of qualities and values and making a conscious decision.

Watercooler Romances

Dating within most companies is frowned upon for obvious reasons. Using company time to make eyes at each other over the watercooler and romantic getaways to the supply room interfere with work. And breakups make for messy interoffice relationships. People who work together often have a lot in common, but when they finish talking company business, conversation can abruptly end.

A Dream Deferred

Exploring new territory works best when you are pursuing your own interests—perhaps reconnecting to a dream you put on hold. Most of us had an idea of what we wanted to be when we grew up—before addiction took over and before others convinced us we didn't want to be what we said we wanted to be. Pay attention to those memories; they're a map back home. They can lead you to activities, groups, and organizations that might awaken and nurture that dream you tucked away for safekeeping. They are sure to put you in the right place to meet people with whom you have something in common.

Here are several questions that will help you reach back through time and find that "dreamer":

- What were three things you loved to do as a kid?
- What did you want to be when you grew up?
- What are the catalogs or stores you find the most interesting to browse through?
- If you had an opportunity to learn something you've always been interested in, what would it be?
- What occupations or lifestyles are you most attracted to?

Expanding into New Social Circles

Enlarging your social circles and meeting new people takes time as well as commitment. Work can feel like the perfect balm for a lonely heart—and so culturally acceptable. Working late might score points with the boss, but if you don't make time for socializing, you won't have time for a relationship. Here are suggestions of activities that can foster your interests and provide opportunities to meet others:

- Go back to school for a degree.
- Take a class in something you're interested in (not necessarily for credit).
- Teach a community education class about a topic you're knowledgeable about.

- Volunteer on a community project: public television fund-raisers, the public library, American Cancer Society, or reading for the blind, to name a few. You can meet social needs and do service work at the same time.
- Work on a political campaign.
- Join a local theater group.
- Check out travel clubs.
- Participate in ethnic or folk dancing groups.
- Join a running or biking club (or hiking, bird watching, snowshoeing, skiing, and so on).

LOCAL GATHERING PLACES

You can meet people at places in your neighborhood, such as the following:

- Coffeehouses
- Bookstores
- Bookstores with coffeehouses
- Film festivals
- Health-food stores
- Open-air markets
- Craft fairs
- Museums
- Libraries
- Laundromats

ORGANIZATIONS AND CLUBS

Here is a list of organizations or activities that might reflect your interests:

- Church groups
- Special-interest groups or clubs such as book clubs, music clubs, or service clubs
- Chamber of commerce or city planning meetings
- Political rallies
- Sporting events of all kinds from Little League to professional sports
- Health clubs
- Walkathons and marathons
- Neighborhood gatherings (walk around your neighborhood with a friend and introduce yourself to your neighbors or organize a small neighborhood party)

FIVE STAR SUGGESTION *****

Friends are a five-star source for meeting new people. Tell them you're dating and that you'd appreciate an introduction if they know someone they think you might be interested in. A variation on this is when a third person helps to get an introduction. This works as follows: When you see someone you would like to know but don't know how to begin, send a buddy over to break the ice. For example, "My friend would like to meet you and wants to know if you're available?" Limit your courier's role to finding out if the person would like to meet you. It's always best to speak for yourself. No one does you better than you.

This is only a partial list of the many opportunities where you can meet interesting people, but it can help put you in the proper mind-set. Before long, you'll be coming up with many ideas of your own. For now, pick one idea from the list and give it a try. If you find it doesn't work for you after a couple of attempts, scratch it off your list and pick another one.

NO WHINERS BEYOND THIS POINT!

For those times when you find your feet are glued to the floor, remember, fear of rejection always goes with doing something new—and that goes double for dating. Besides, there is a good chance your fear might come true; you may get voted off the island. But you've made a courageous decision to grow, so stand up straight, shoulders back, and no whining!

THE OLD FLY-ON-THE-WALL TRICK

The best approach can be summed up in two words: be real. Rigorous honesty is at the heart of the Twelve Step recovery program, so is sharing hope, strength, and experience. Be honest, friendly, and positive, and you can't go wrong. At the very least you'll be practicing your principles. As previously stated, landing a date isn't the end result of this project. Dating is about you learning more about yourself, developing your social skills, and getting out into the world.

A favorite technique that almost always works to ease discomfort and get you going on your dating plan is to become the observer in your mind—the fly on the wall. It's the opposite of checking out. You're present but with room to have the experience without getting critical or collapsing into it. It's the observer's job to pay attention to you—to notice how you are feeling—and not to take notes on the other person. Be sure the observer is on your side, offering plenty of positive encouragement in a friendly voice.

Believe It or Not, Ripley

Believe it or not, a person tells you who he is in the first two minutes of conversation. The problem is that we are so focused on what we want to hear, don't want to hear, or what to say next, we don't hear what is being said. Later, when something has gone wrong and we go over those first few sentences, we realize the person told us exactly what to expect. Following are a few red flags that might spare you an unnecessary surprise. Encourage your "fly on the wall" to read through the list and to keep it in mind when out on a date.

Red Flags

Be concerned if a date exhibits any of the following behaviors:

- Is dressed in a costume and it's not Halloween
- Is married or involved with someone
- Has an alcohol, other drug, sex, gambling, or other addictive problem
- Has anger, rage, or a violent streak
- Hates or is in love with his mother, her father, or a former partner
- Asks to borrow fifty dollars on your first date
- Hears no and thinks go
- Makes demeaning or sarcastic remarks about the opposite sex

- Belittles you or others
- Needs to control the times, dates, and places where you meet (micromanages)
- Has more than twenty-three cats
- Is over forty and sleeps on a relative's couch
- Is carrying a placard saying "The End Is Near"

CONVERSATION TIPS

Getting a conversation going can feel nerve-racking, but here are a few techniques that can reduce the intimidation factor and yield good results. Practice asking open-ended questions rather than those that can be answered by a simple yes or no. Here is an example showing the difference between open-ended and closed questions:

Closed: Is this your first class?

Open-ended: What made you decide to take this class?
Open-ended: What made you consider this school?
Open-ended: What do you know about this instructor?

It takes some thought and practice to learn how to phrase questions this way, but the results are worth it. Most people enjoy being asked to say something about themselves. You'll get a conversation going when you make room for it by giving the other person a chance to talk.

Compliments can be good conversation starters, if they're real. If someone has caught your attention, figure out why and let this person know. For example, "You have a great laugh." "You have a wonderful smile." "You have a nice voice." *Caution:* Don't go below the neck!

Conversation No-Nos

- No jokes
- No pat lines (For example, "Where have you been all my life?")

Topic No-Nos

- Sex
- Other people
- Business
- Religion
- Politics

Other No-Nos

- No hang-ups—calling and hanging up when someone answers
- No weird messages on the machine
- No drive-bys
- No monopolizing the conversation
- No continuing if it isn't working

In the event that the other person does any of the above no-nos and it irritates you, you may add it to your red flag list or blow it off figuring she hasn't read the *Easy Does It Dating Guide*, in which case you might suggest it to her.

We generally spend way too much time focused on talking when good communication begins with careful listening. The popular adage reminds us we have two ears and only one mouth. Practice paying attention to every word a person is saying without thinking of what you'll say next. When he finishes, give an honest response instead of rushing into a comparable story.

For example, your friend tells you about a harrowing ride across town in rush-hour traffic in an attempt to keep an appointment. Conversation-friendly responses include:

- "It sounds like you really got into a mess."
- "After all that, did you make your appointment on time?"

Conversation-stopping responses include:

- Dueling banjos response: "That's nothing; let me tell you about the time . . ."
- Toxic teacher response: "I always leave early if I'm going to an important appointment."
- Hey-dummy response: "If you go down the freeway to the third exit and turn right, you avoid all that traffic."

It's the other person's topic, not yours. Listen to what the story is about for that person and give your honest response. You don't have to match stories, teach a lesson, or give advice. After the subject has been exhausted, it's your turn to bring up the next topic.

Rapport Building

Sales seminars teach quick rapport-building techniques for increasing business. If you use any of them, choose carefully. Some are based on common sense and can correctly be considered social skills while others border on manipulation. You're going for honest and above board. Making eye contact and turning your body toward the person you are talking with, using a friendly tone of voice, and keeping the conversation light and positive are straightforward, friendly mannerisms that work.

Some Dos and Don'ts

- *Do* look people in the eye.
- *Don't* glare.

- *Do* smile.
- *Don't* grin like a cat who swallowed the canary.

- *Do* use open body language.
- *Don't* act sexy.

- Men: *Don't* stare at body parts.
- Women: *Don't* give that lost little girl look and twirl your hair.

Admitting that you are nervous or that you're not accustomed to approaching someone you don't know is being honest. Both reveal a bit of vulnerability without suggesting you're inept. This opens the way for further talk. It takes a little vulnerability in order to relate to someone even in a light conversation, but keep in mind that a detailed discussion of your flaws closes the door to anyone who has any sense.

FLIRTING IS OKAY, BUT DON'T ROLL OVER

Question: When is a flirt not a flirt?
Answer: When she crosses a very thin line.

Note: If you find the whole idea of flirting a demeaning turnoff and would rather die than do it, you might want to fast-forward to the next topic. Others may find it interesting to know that many people flirt unconsciously when they are attracted to someone.

For a lot of people, flirting is fun, lighthearted, playful, and shows confidence. It relies on charm and appeal. It tells the other person you might be interested but suggests nothing past that. A come-on crosses the line and sends a sexual signal. Rather than confidence, it gives the impression you can be had and screams poor boundaries.

Whether it's a flirt or a come-on depends on how you do it and whom you are flirting with. Save flirting for the person you know and are interested in; flirt with your date, not your date's best friend.

Successful flirting techniques include sharing a "secret" such as you're dying for an ice-cream cone or you can't wait to get your bare feet in the grass—not that you drowned your brother's cat.

A study of women's flirting behavior shows that almost all use the same or similar techniques—a universal flirting language that probably originated among our cave-dwelling sisters. Smiling tops the list, followed by eye contact. Women first open their eyes wide, which subconsciously signals something important is about to happen. This is followed by lowering her eyelids, tilting her head to the side, and looking away, extending a subtle, demure invitation.

Men's flirting follows some of the same patterns as women's but is opposite in a significant way: generally speaking, women signal their receptivity, and men show their assertiveness. Of course, this doesn't include yelling "Hey, baby!" out of the truck window. Men make eye contact, smile, and focus attention on the person they are hoping to impress. They will listen attentively, nod in agreement, smile, and laugh frequently. Posture sends signals too, and when a man is interested he tends to come to "attention," squaring his shoulders, standing bigger and taller, holding his head up. Sooner or later, he'll unconsciously give indications of his financial prowess, actually showing money or referencing his job or his car.

Note: Lie detector tests record physical responses generated by lying. Likewise, Pinocchio's nose gave him away—and yours can too. The tip of the nose actually engorges with blood when we're lying. That's why people often rub their nose when fabricating stories. Another call for rigorous honesty!

Moving the Ball down the Field

Nothing about dating is carved in stone anymore. In male-female dating, the traditional way puts the responsibility on the man to initiate conversation, get the phone number, ask for the date, figure out the details, pick up his date, pay the check, and see the woman home. When you look at it this way, women's liberation might seem more appealing to men out there who haven't already embraced it.

Nowadays, a woman can feel comfortable initiating the conversation and making all the calls from start to finish. Dating arrangements can also be done through a mutual agreement. Some take a cue from the gay community, where unless it's stated up-front, whoever does the inviting usually takes responsibility for setting things up and picking up the check. The score can be evened in future dates. Using an honest, straightforward approach will probably be the most comfortable and bring the best results for you.

If your conversation flows fairly well, and it's obvious you're both showing interest, you can say something such as "I'm really enjoying talking with you, and I'd like the chance to continue our conversation. Would you be available to meet for coffee next week?" If you get a positive response, go ahead and establish a time. If you don't make plans at that time but are interested in doing so later, you may wish to exchange phone numbers. Generally speaking, when a man asks for a woman's number, the most cautious thing is to offer his and give her the option of giving hers. For example, "I'd love to see you again. Can I give you my number, or would you feel okay giving me yours?" If you remember the discussion on boundaries in chapter 4, women are more vulnerable than men in our society. Whether it is politically correct or not, it generally doesn't work for a woman to be too forward when talking with a man, particularly one she doesn't know. It is advisable for women to exercise caution when giving out their phone number or address to anyone they don't know.

Regardless of whether you're a man or a woman, if you are being honest and polite, you'll leave an impression of sincerity and probably won't regret asking for a phone number even if you don't get a call later. If someone asks for your number and you know you don't want that person to call, politely and firmly decline: "No, thanks." This can be expanded to include "but thanks for asking," if you feel like it. But avoid giving a double message, leaving the person uncertain of what you just said.

Note: Men and women live in different time zones when it comes to the phrase, "I'd like to call you." A woman will typically go home and expect the phone to be ringing when she opens the front door. She'll check her machine often and regularly. After about four days, she thinks, *Yeah, right.* When he does call, she's a bit edgy. Men think in terms of a couple of weeks, figuring that calling right away might seem like they're too needy or pressuring her.

Asking for a Date

This is a good time for the fly-on-the-wall trick. Observe how cool and confident you are. Avoid hedging your bet by using that nebulous *sometime*—as in "Do you want to go out *sometime?*" Have a place and a couple of dates in mind. If the answer is no, realize it isn't about you; the person doesn't even know you.

Self-Evaluation

If the answer is no, when you get home, sit down and have a talk with the fly. Use the form that follows to discover how you felt when you were turned down. Separate the facts from your feelings and decide if you can handle it or not.

Fact: I said . . .

_____

_____

_____

_____

Feeling: I was feeling . . .

_____

_____

_____

_____

Fact: He or she said . . .

_____

_____

_____

_____

Feeling: I felt . . .

_____

_____

_____

_____

Analyze the exchange with the following questions:

- Were your feelings similar to the ones you uncovered during your dating Fourth Step?
- Were there "tactical" errors on your part—meaning previous indicators that the person might not say yes? Could it just be life on life's terms?
- Did the experience cause you so much trouble you can't go on dating?

FIVE BEST PICKS FOR PLACE

When your efforts have paid off and you're setting up a date, here are a few suggestions on selecting a place to go:

- Pick a place where conversation will be easy.
- Pick a location that's easy to find (meet there).
- Pick a casual place that calls for casual dress.
- Pick a place that's affordable.
- Pick something you both enjoy doing.

FAVORITE FIRST-DATE SUGGESTIONS

Your local tourist bureau is a great resource for finding events in your hometown. It will have brochures advertising many interesting things to do such as walking tours, free concerts, events at local parks, and more. Here's a list to get you started:

- Walks
- Museums
- Aquariums
- Parks—not remote ones
- Art galleries
- Coffeehouses
- Casual restaurant for breakfast or lunch
- Local craft fairs
- Outside markets
- Antique malls

Lesser Favorites

The following places or events are acceptable venues but are not preferred for first dates because they aren't favorable for carrying on conversations:

- Sporting events
- Sports bars
- Concerts
- Movies

Not Recommended for First Dates

Avoid these events on first dates, or early on in a relationship, as they can be too emotionally loaded:

- Christmas parties
- Thanksgiving dinner
- New Year's Eve parties

- any function on Valentine's Day
- Weddings
- Family reunions
- Dinner at your place or at your date's place

RESTAURANT TIPS

Restaurants are often the top choice for a place to meet on a first date. Restaurants are safe, comfortable, and cozy, and food is friendly and nurturing and lends itself to good conversation. Here are some further suggestions to consider if you decide on a restaurant for your first date:

- Consider meeting for a meal other than dinner. Dinner is generally more formal and is more likely to make both of you nervous. Lunch, breakfast, or even meeting for coffee is more casual and comfortable.
- Choose a medium-priced place.
- Order something easy to eat; save cracked lobster for later.
- Eat slowly and enjoy your meal (put your fork down once in a while and sit back and relax).
- Use good manners but don't be stiff.
- If you spill something, don't make it into a federal case. Just spot clean your shirtfront and let the server clean the table.
- Be polite to the server.
- Tip well.

Men: It's still a good idea to ask if your date would like a ride. If you are meeting somewhere at night, it's nice to ask if you can see her home—just to be safe. However, it's best to meet at the location; this avoids any awkward moments if she doesn't feel comfortable letting you know where she lives. One woman said she would never ever let anyone pick her up. She had a negative experience once and escaped unharmed but was ever so grateful she had her own car. Also to be considered is that clumsy moment at the door—to kiss or not to kiss. The latter is the safer bet. A handshake or a very brief hug (cousin style) is enough for now.

Women: If you live at the opposite end of the county and it's going to be an inconvenience to be picked up or brought home, talk about it. Maybe there's another way of doing it, such as going somewhere closer or meeting during the day. Spend time getting the details arranged so you both feel comfortable now rather than running into trouble later.

CREATIVE FINANCIAL PLANNING

The matter of who pays is another place where the rules have changed. In our corner of the world, money is power—and it's pretty hard not to be influenced by it. The following story shows how two women worked out the dynamics of different incomes (it works the same in male-female dating):

Laura discovered that when Emily paid for everything, it triggered her codependency. It was not anything Emily was doing; it was purely Laura's own issues. Laura found she was going to movies she didn't like and eating in restaurants she wouldn't necessarily go to if she were out with friends or paying her own way. She explained her feelings to Emily, and they reached an agreement.

Emily's income was higher, and she liked to go to expensive restaurants and could afford theater tickets that Laura couldn't buy. Emily was sensitive to what her friend was experiencing but didn't want to be limited by Laura's budget either. They decided to divide the expenses proportionally to reflect their individual incomes—Laura paid about a third of the bill. Sometimes Laura would cook meals with food Emily provided.

The point is you can set things up to work for you. Just talk about it before the check comes, and if you're splitting it, split it in half or by a third, not item by item.

Using a healthy approach to dating, where most of the surprises have been removed, might seem a bit dull at first glance, particularly if you've always dated high-risk style. Hopefully you'll discover some planning creates safety and comfort. Safety doesn't rule out spontaneity but puts both people on equal footing and makes room for it. Generally speaking, the more comfortable you feel, the easier it is to have conversation and the better time you have. Of course, there are occasions when even a healthy person can be just plain boring. But confusing boring with safety is not part of the healthy dating agenda.

WHAT TO EXPECT ON THE FIRST THREE DATES

Here's an idea of what to expect (from you and from the other person) on the first three dates:

- Punctuality: arrive at the appointed place on time.
- Nice presentation: be clean and groomed, smile, and offer a friendly greeting such as "It's great to see you," "You look very nice," or "I've been looking forward to this."
- Good manners toward each other and toward others.

- Pleasant and agreeable conversation.
- No cell phones unless children or emergency rooms are involved. Even then, excuse yourself from the table and keep it brief.
- Mutual decision making about plans, including approximately when you both need to go home.
- A time limit on the date: avoid letting the occasion run on and on and on. . . . Save some for next time.
- No apologies! If you find you are apologizing a lot, stop. Compose yourself and settle down. If you're on the receiving end of endless apologies, perhaps you can encourage the person to relax rather than saying "That's okay" continuously.
- Mutual sharing of stories, taking turns without trying to top the other's story.
- No sexual innuendos, invitations, or advances.

FOLLOW-UP AND ACCOUNTABILITY

If everything has gone well, regardless of who did the asking and arranging, it's polite to call the next day and say you had a nice time—but avoid a long phone conversation. Save your thoughts for when you are together. If you did the asking on the first round, you might want to see if your date sets the next one in motion. In due time, go back over your list of expectations, paying special attention to any nonnegotiable items you might have ignored. Make notes and talk with your relationship sponsor about it to keep perspective and hold the line. This isn't a grading card for your date; it's about your ability to hold your boundaries.

Note: Remember, it takes a conscious effort not to slide back into old behaviors until you establish new ones.

There is a saying in recovery that if you're not on your

calendar, you aren't showing up in your life. We suggest you put your personal activities on your daily planner, including your recovery meetings, exercise regime, and any other routine gatherings you attend. Make sure you are keeping your regular meeting schedule, making only minor adjustments to accommodate your dating schedule. The same is true of maintaining service work and socializing in the fellowship. This is where accountability with a sponsor and home group is valuable.

Following are six ways to know when you're disappearing off your radar screen, accommodating others at the expense of your recovery, or beginning to isolate:

_____ You've missed the meeting you don't ever miss—more than once.

_____ You've changed or removed engagements that were already on your calendar to accommodate your date—more than once.

_____ You've fallen off your exercise schedule or have started skipping grocery shopping or other self-care activities.

_____ You don't tell any of your friends you're seeing someone.

_____ Your friends have forgotten what you look like, and you can't remember their phone numbers.

_____ You've forgotten what you look like and can't remember your own phone number.

Summary Points

- There are lots of places to go and things to do in recovery that develop your interests and allow you to meet people.

- Honesty is the best policy when it comes to your approach, asking for a date, and all other conversations.
- There aren't any hard-and-fast rules about who asks, who pays, transportation, or any other parts of dating. The trend is toward making decisions together.
- There is always a risk involved in learning a new skill. You've got a good support system in recovery; be sure and use it.

The next chapter covers the HOW (honest, open, and willing) of dating. You'll have a chance to make your dating wish list and get the Easy Does It spin on intimacy, emotions, and commitment. There are even some suggestions for fighting fair, to help with those inevitable differences of opinion.

Chapter Seven ✳

The HOW of Dating and Relating

- Sharing or spilling your guts: the wisdom to know the difference.
- Is list making spiritually correct?
- What you won't get in a relationship.
- Nuances and complexities of intimacy.

The acronym HOW stands for honest, open, and willing and describes what it takes to grow and change in recovery. This acronym will also help cover the basics of HOW to date.

First let's review the main points of the first phase of dating and relating: single and dating.

Review: Landing a date isn't the end point of this book or of your quest. If you think about the first phase of dating as a time of discovery or even a shopping trip, you're in the *process*. Later, after you've learned the ropes, you can decide if you're ready to look for a partner and invest in a relationship. The choices you're learning to make will allow you to grow from dating to relating and eventually to mating—Easy Does It style. Now let's see about launching you on your journey.

HONEST: MAKING A LIST AND CHECKING IT TWICE

The experts say that love is the result of a series of choices. Combining this technique with the time-tested marketing principle of list making can help you design a dating plan.

You probably don't have *too* much trouble when it comes to picking out a place to live, a car, or something to wear to a special occasion—and most likely you don't buy the first thing you see. Rather, you probably check out several houses, try on various outfits, or take as many test-drives around the block as you possibly can. Yet you may hesitate to put that much energy into selecting a person you might end up with for a lot longer.

Real estate agents advise customers to write down the things they want in a house, including factors such as availability, style, and affordability and to get as specific as possible. There's no such thing as a perfect house or a perfect relationship, but making conscious decisions about what's absolutely necessary and what is negotiable is important for success. The key is preparing your list *before* your emotions enter the picture. When emotions fire up, practicality often takes a backseat.

Your Appreciation Dinner

The first test of honesty is to make a list of your qualities— the things you most like about yourself. Hopefully you are far enough along in your recovery to enjoy a little self-celebrating. In fact, consider turning the process into an appreciation dinner; invite friends and ask for their help as you claim the good stuff you bring to the table. They see things that you can't. Here is a sample list to get you started.

I appreciate my

___ honesty
___ dedication to recovery
___ interest in growing and knowing more about myself
___ willingness to be of service to others
___ ability to be self-supporting
___ humor

___ flexibility
___ love of freedom
___ desire to share my journey with another

Descriptive Paragraphs

When you've made your list, prioritize the top five attributes (what you like most about yourself) and write a couple of paragraphs about them. Include your best traits, a physical description, hobbies and interests, kinds of music you like, plans for the future, and so on. You might imagine you're writing a description for a singles ad, but you're not going to mail it. The purpose of this exercise is to make sure you approach dating with a positive attitude about yourself.

Write a Gratitude Letter

Referring back to your list of qualities and the descriptive paragraphs above, write a thank-you letter to your Higher Power expressing gratitude for the gifts you've been given—specifically mentioning each gift. Acknowledging the good job your Higher Power did in designing your soul is a guaranteed way of getting past any leftover unhealed self-esteem issues.

Set Your Intention

Turn back to Chapter 3: Getting Different Results and write down the vision statement you composed that describes your intention in dating. A sample vision statement (also included in chapter 3) follows: *I would meet new people, have fun dating, and eventually have a healthy romantic relationship while continuing to develop my spiritual life and grow in my recovery.*

Make Conscious Contact

Owning your natural, healthy desire to date and getting clear about what you want is taking responsibility for yourself.

It's an adult thing and is spiritually correct. However, beware of getting caught up in old patterns and ideas, such as self-will run riot. If you find yourself backsliding, quickly correct yourself.

You're in a process—doing the footwork, being honest, suiting up and showing up, as the saying goes. As you no doubt know by now, there is an art to wanting something and taking steps toward your desire, while not triggering your addiction or attempting to control the results. Your recovery program tells you to do your part, let go of the results, and surrender to God's will. It leaves room for your Higher Power to get involved. A good way to resist taking control is through the Third Step prayer from the Big Book of Alcoholics Anonymous, which follows. Or use a prayer or meditation of your own choosing.

> God, I offer myself to Thee—to build with me and to do with me as Thou wilt. Relieve me of the bondage of self, that I may better do Thy will. Take away my difficulties, that victory over them may bear witness to those I would help of Thy Power, Thy Love, and Thy Way of life. May I do Thy will always! (63)

The Big Book reminds us God wants us to be happy, joyous, and free. It's good to be mindful of the order of business here. You are claiming happiness, joy, and freedom as your spiritual birthright through your relationship with a Higher Power—*not through dating*. If you don't experience these qualities within yourself at least a good portion of the time, you won't get them from a relationship; relationships are mirrors, reflecting our own qualities back to us.

Your Wish List

You were honest about what you have to offer. Now be honest about what you are looking for in another person. The list is to help you stay mindful of what you are looking for in another. It's not a list for Santa. Qualities you thought were cool when you were practicing your addiction may very well leave you cold in recovery. Likewise, qualities you thought were dull and boring might seem safe and comfortable when you're clean and sober. It doesn't hurt to have a written reminder. Get as specific as you want, including your ideal physical description, and make your list as long as it needs to be. Go back over chapter 4 on boundaries to see if anything needs to be added. Later, as you prioritize your list, the most important qualities will surface.

Here is an example of qualities others have listed as preferences in dating partners:

____ Available
____ Kind
____ Generous
____ Honest
____ Supportive
____ Humorous
____ Compassionate
____ Flexible
____ Imaginative
____ Romantic
____ Likes outdoors
____ Self-aware
____ Spiritually aware
____ Self-supporting
____ Nonsmoking
____ Nonaddicted
____ If addicted: clean and working a program

Mark the nonnegotiable qualities—your deal breakers—remembering availability and honesty are always nonnegotiable. Next, prioritize your list and select the top five qualities. No one will have everything you're looking for, but this gives you a working plan of your own design with room for negotiation. Hang on to your lists and other materials as a reference. (Check exercise 2 in appendix A for the Five-Point Quick Evaluation form.)

Open: The Capacity for Intimacy

Intimacy is a trust that gradually develops between two people who spend time together. Intimacy begins with getting to know another through sharing stories; it progresses into emotional intimacy, the world of shared feelings, and finally to physical and sexual intimacy, which are discussed in chapter 8.

You'll stay in the storytelling phase of intimacy-building during the single and dating stage. Conversation centers around where you grew up, your childhood dog, the type of music you like, movies you've seen or books you've read, favorite sports teams, concerts you've attended, and so on. If things don't click at this early stage, it's easy to opt out with no hurt feelings on either side.

Note: These early conversations aren't the time to tell all regarding your childhood trauma, your risky drinking and drugging behavior, or how hard you've worked in recovery. It isn't that you're trying to hide anything, but even Mother Teresa would be thrown for a loop when hearing those stories before getting to know you better. It's like the seven-year-old who asks her parents where she came from. They launch into an elaborate discussion of the birds and bees, taking the child through conception, nine months of pregnancy, and a difficult birth. When they finish, the child's eyes are as big as baseballs when she says, "Oh! Janie came from Cleveland." So for now, when you're exchanging histories, just say you're from Cleveland.

As you read about emotional intimacy, you'll see why we suggest waiting before including it in your dating life. It gets complex fast. For now, just relax and enjoy a preview of what's to come later in your relationship quest.

Moving from Dating to Relating

The dynamics of the early stages of dating change abruptly when emotions enter the picture. The goal in the *Easy Does It Dating Guide* is to avoid emotional intimacy until you have completed the shopping-but-not-buying part of the process as described earlier in the book. Later, when you and your potential partner make a conscious decision to build a relationship, you enter the time of emotional intimacy. Emotional intimacy quickly leads to emotional bonding, so you want to make sure your selection of a potential partner meets your criteria before bonding. It's a horse-and-cart kind of thing. The more care you use in selecting a partner, the better the chances of the relationship working and the less emotional pain if it does not work out.

What Is Intimacy?

We hear the word *intimacy* a lot, usually followed by a sharp intake of breath and a shudder. It's one of those mysterious terms most of us don't clearly grasp, but we intuitively sense its power. Intimacy is more than sharing stories and spending time together, and to be intimate we don't have to have sex or be married. So what is intimacy?

Intimacy, as the word implies, has to do with your inner workings—your emotions. In his book *Addictive Relationships: Why Love Goes Wrong in Recovery*, Terence Gorski defines intimacy quite simply as the "ability to identify your thoughts and emotions and share them with another person" (8–9). He goes on to say that you need to listen while the other person does the same thing. The conversation thus begins, gradually deepening and exploring more inner territory. He's describing yet another process.

Gorski's definition of intimacy is clear enough, but a relationship doesn't suddenly endow you with these skills. You have to have the capacity to identify your thoughts and emotions and to interpret them appropriately without arguing with yourself. When you've mastered the process within, you can take it on the road.

Science used to believe we could be objective—separate thought from emotion. This idea has proven to be false. We now know there isn't an objective reality; our emotions influence our thoughts and vice versa. However, we grew up in a world where thoughts had more credibility than emotions. This is one of the key reasons why relationships are challenging. Thinking and feeling are two parts of one system. Each plays an equally important role and both have to work together.

Emotions Are Like Weather

Because addiction is largely about mood tampering (adjusting and fixing feelings), recovering people aren't always at their best in the emotional department. It might be helpful to think of emotions as weather fronts: they move through your area. Weather is important, but despite the meteorologist's pronouncements of "good" and "bad" weather, it really has no morality. Emotions, like the weather, are important but have no morality. They are simply natural phenomena—human impulses and reactions. It's what you do with your emotions that matters.

Emotions are *real*; they are *really* happening. They give you accurate information about what is going on inside of you. However, a conclusion you draw based solely on emotions may or may not give you an accurate analysis of what's happening on the outside. As was mentioned in the discussion of boundaries in chapter 4, an emotion might signal you to pay attention. For example, you might be frightened when the wind rattles the shutters. This doesn't necessarily mean danger. Your fear is telling you to check things out. It might be reminding you of another time when a similar noise turned out to be dangerous. Upon investigation, you may find it is nothing more than a banging shutter. Of course, your investigation might also alert you to real danger. You have to pay attention to internal warning signals *and* check things out.

Wisdom to Know the Difference

The brain has both an internal information system (the feeling/sensing function) and an external information system (the analyzing/thinking function). Ideally the two systems work together to help you know who you are and to help you operate successfully in the world.

Emotions are impulses happening in the right hemisphere of the brain based on sensory information—things you've heard, seen, smelled, tasted, or touched, sometimes without conscious awareness. Emotions tell us what's happening inside. The impulse is transmitted to the other hemisphere, the brain's thinking function, through a part of the brain called the corpus callosum to get a reading. The analyzing/thinking function tells us what's happening outside. (*Note:* The left brain doesn't analyze the emotion. It analyzes the outside reality.)

The interpretation of the external information travels back across the "wiring" to the right hemisphere where it generates an emotional response. The response might be experienced as a calming down; your feeling side might agree with the interpretation; or the feeling might intensify, in which case it's saying, *something's wrong—check things out further.* Emotions are felt and thoughts are re-evaluated, adjusted, and changed. This inner conversation can go back and forth for hours, days, or even weeks.

Note: Healthy thinking depends on not overruling emotions or disregarding them, but taking them seriously and working with them. Likewise, healthy emotions rely on the thinking mind to interpret the external world.

This informational system is a living, breathing process—a creative conversation full of give and take. Neither function has the last word; things are always being negotiated, assessed, checked, and balanced. A healthy system depends on having a mixture of sensitivity and flexibility. The process isn't difficult or confusing when you respect both sides of the discussion and don't rush it. At some point the feeling part and the thinking part find an agreement; your head and stomach settle down, and you feel peaceful.

Often we're not conscious of this inner conversation, but we definitely feel the results of it. For instance, you might be unable to sleep well for a couple of weeks, feeling anxious but not sure what it's about. You suddenly remember to mail the rent check you stuck behind the car visor, and before you know it you're sleeping well again. You didn't consciously know that taking care of this business was related to your anxiety or you would've done it sooner, but your feelings were prompting you to take care of it and your thoughts finally caught up. Emotions are chemicals. Unexpressed emotions stay in their chemical state in the body as physical feelings. Think of the times when you've said someone is a pain in the neck! Unexpressed emotions are often experienced as stomach cramps, headaches, or shortness of breath. An example: You may notice that every time you schedule a date with a certain guy you get a cold sore or a headache. Your thoughts have been struggling with your feelings. You know he's not right, but you see him because it's convenient and then you get sick. Finally, your thoughts and feelings agree about the guy; you stop seeing him and get healthy.

Repressed emotions complicate matters, making it more difficult to know what is happening now and what is a memory being stimulated. But no matter when the emotions originated, getting them out in the open is key. Expressing emotions includes everything from talking about them with a friend to jumping up and down flapping your arms. You can scream, dance, paint, write songs about emotions—anything but pretend they aren't happening.

As we become more attuned to this conversation, feeling our feelings and checking things out, we're coming to greater self-awareness.

Here is the formula: we feel emotions and analyze the external world; we don't try to analyze our feelings or interpret the world by our emotions. When an emotion is denied, repressed, or overruled, thinking gets distorted. Likewise, we get "out of touch" with our external reality (the world) if we don't think our emotions through. It is not a case of one over the other but of always finding a place of agreement. This internal model of balance becomes the model we use for relationships.

Reality: Check and Double-Check

In every relationship, emotions inevitably get triggered by the other person's behavior. When it happens, it isn't clear whether the person is doing something to us or we're doing it to ourselves. It's good to remember that when you think someone is making you to feel a certain way, it may or may not be true. It may be that something he is doing reminds you of a past event. Once the chemicals of the unexpressed emotion start flowing, it's hard to tell the difference between the past and the present. Sometimes the person is behaving in a troubling way and you are truly receiving vital signals. Other times the person is an innocent bystander caught in the crosshairs of your emotional memories. Intimacy requires a high degree of self-knowledge, skill, and a lot of reality checks.

Following is an example of how you can get completely offtrack when inner dialogue doesn't take place:

1. You feel lonely. This feeling is telegraphed to the left hemisphere for a reading on the external reality.
2. Your partner is out of town. Your thinking assumes it's your partner's absence that is causing your loneliness.
3. You don't check this out with your feelings, assuming your thinking mind knows the whole answer.
4. You tell your partner that she isn't spending enough time with you.
5. Your partner has a predictable reaction and pulls away.
6. Your feeling of abandonment intensifies. It is now being reinforced by your partner's reaction to incorrect information. Your case is building. You have "proof"! (As you can see, it is getting complicated, and it isn't over with yet.)

In order to bring yourself back to reality, you need to check in with both sides of your brain and see all the possibilities. Your partner may actually be emotionally abandoning you. Or your loneliness may be an indication that you have begun to abandon yourself and are becoming emotionally dependent on your partner. Either case has to be addressed for the relationship to be healthy.

As you sort things out, keep in mind that unresolved childhood stuff gets played out in intimate relationships. You may unconsciously attempt to get your partner to be your emotional parent, or you may attempt to emotionally parent your partner. The truth is, it's your responsibility to meet your emotional needs—with very few exceptions. Emotional partners sign on to be supportive of one another—not to be primary caregivers.

Intimacy requires self-knowledge. Naming your feelings and thinking them through, writing them down, or talking them over with a friend brings insight. It's important to know whether the feeling is an old one being triggered or whether it's a new one being generated by the relationship. If you discover your loneliness has to do with your partner's absence, you may want to talk about it together (this is you taking care of you). You may have different expectations about togetherness. You have the option of asking if she would like to spend more time with you and of figuring out how that can be arranged. Other options are to call a friend or go to a meeting. Finding reasonable options is problem solving with your adult mind.

Respectful Listening

Intimacy depends on not being triggered by another's emotions or getting caught up in another's reality. It calls for nonjudgmental listening. We can mistake our role in intimacy as being that of a teacher—telling the other person what we think they should feel, do, or know about themselves. Intimacy is really about discovering more about yourself. Listening while a person explores his inner world without making assumptions, judging, or trying to know the answers conveys a sense of trust. You are letting the person know you believe he'll find what he's looking for—his truth.

A Book in a Windstorm

For recovering people, emotional intimacy can be like reading a book in a windstorm—you blink and miss twenty pages of dialogue. It goes something like this:

Partner #1: I'm feeling lonely.
Partner #2: I did not!

Partner #1 doesn't know that partner #2 has a history around the word *lonely* and terrible feelings of having to emotionally caretake a lonely parent. The word is loaded with old baggage, making conversation out of the question.
With practice, it might go something like this:

Partner #1: I'm feeling lonely.
Partner #2: (Has an unusually strong reaction) It's not
my fault you don't have any friends!

Impartial observer: (Hmmm. Where did that come
from?)

Partner #1: (Takes it and runs) I've got more friends
than you have!

Partner #2 could then react by itemizing both sets of friends. Both can then argue about whose friend Marjorie *really* is, or they can nip it in the bud by learning a few simple techniques.
When you realize your partner is having a reaction that doesn't match the scenery, you can calmly ask, "What's going on when you hear me say I'm lonely?"
Your partner might say, "When you say you're lonely, I feel responsible, like I'm supposed to take care of that, and I can't. . . . I feel like a failure!"

Again, you have options as to how you respond. If you aren't reacting to your "stuff," you might realize your partner has just stepped into the past and ask if she would like to explore where that feeling of failure is coming from.

There are many different responses to a person's trip into yesteryear, and this is only one example. The point is to be present enough to catch when either of you is reacting to the past rather than being in the moment.

With a sharp ear, a slow tongue, and practice you can discover all sorts of things about yourself and the other person. You might want to look at exercise 3 in appendix A for a self-evaluation of your intimacy skills.

Trust: Don't Rush to Judge

The following tip can save you hundreds of hours of grief and thousands of dollars of therapy. It can also make you a gifted conversationalist, which means being a good listener. The tip: Train your mind to avoid making snap judgments, and teach it to ask questions instead. That goes for dealing with yourself as well as with others. Following are more useful tactics to help you be a careful listener even during a charged conversation:

- Avoid feeling attacked or responsible for your partner's emotions.
- Avoid saying, "I don't see why you feel like that. There is really no reason for you to feel that way."
- Instead, say something such as "I can see you're angry. Can you tell me more about what's going on for you?"
- Ask the person what he needs right now.
- Be honest about what you can take on. Most of the time being a supportive listener without trying to solve your partner's feelings is enough. We get

defensive when we think we have to do something we don't want to do—such as fix someone.

- Learn to use encouraging language that keeps you out of the fixing mode and tells the other that you believe she can do it. For example, "I know you'll find the answer. I am looking forward to hearing how you resolve this. I can see this is important to you, and I know you'll succeed. I can imagine you finding exactly what you're looking for."

Intimacy and Commitment

Commitment is another one of those charged words for which we often lack a definition, and of course, there are many ways of defining it. Intimacy and commitment are inextricably connected. Commitment can be understood as our willingness to engage emotionally (with self or other) and develop the skills required for satisfying intimate conversations. Intimacy is when we go deeper into our process, which is a commitment to grow spiritually and come to increasing levels of consciousness. When we are intimately committed to another, we sign on to be present while this person does the same.

For Better or for Worse . . .

A successful relationship can sometimes be defined more by how well partners negotiate the rough places than the smooth ones. There will inevitably be times when your partner doesn't see things the same way or feel the same way as you about issues.

When partners are problem solving together (otherwise known as arguing), another layer gets added. In addition to your emotional reactions, your partner will be having reactions too. Things can heat up pretty fast. Remember that disagreements are normal, and fighting is a part of close relationships, but it isn't okay to fight dirty. No name-calling, no getting physical, no silent treatment or leaving. If one of you gets too tense (or hot under the collar) or begins to shut down, suspend the discussion, but let the other know what's happening and when you'll be back. For example, "I'm about to lose my temper. I need to take a break. Can we pick this up later tonight?" or "I am shutting down. I've got to go in the other room and breathe. I'll come back in a few minutes."

Generally speaking, if you are in your adult mind, you can do this successfully. When the child part of you becomes involved, the discussion degenerates fast. This is usually when the name-calling starts. However, if the parent part of you takes over, you'll enact your family-of-origin pattern—becoming abusive or withholding or teaching the other a lesson—whatever game was played at home.

Save the Surprises for Christmas

When something about your partner is bothering you, it's best to schedule talks rather than rely on the element of surprise, as in an ambush. Let your partner know you need to talk as soon as possible. Agree on when, where, and about how much time you can both spend. Operate within the established framework as much as possible. When something comes up that has to be addressed right then and there, let your partner know it is an emergency, but be careful not to overuse your emergency button.

When emotions are pounding, they make you feel that something has to be done about the situation *right now!* In truth, the more intense the emotion, the more you should wait. If the house isn't on fire, sit still and breathe until your emotions calm down. You can train yourself to feel your emotions without always trying to change something outside of yourself. (See exercise 4 in appendix A on deep breathing.)

Something else to keep in mind when considering start-ing an impromptu discussion is the acronym HALT, which means don't let yourself get too hungry, angry, lonely, or tired. This principle applies in relationship discussions too. It is a good idea to delay talking when you're susceptible to any of these.

When you consider the fine points of emotional intimacy, you can see it takes time, sensitivity, love, trust, and a big commitment to each other and to being in the moment. Twelve Step spirituality, as well as most spiritual traditions all over the world, identifies those exact qualities, remind-ing us that the pursuit of them *is* the journey. It may take a lifetime to get there.

WILLING: MATTERS OF COMPATIBILITY

Willingness can be looked at as compatibility. No matter how willing you are to overlook basic areas where the two of you don't jive, the relationship probably still won't work without a certain level of compatibility. Let's look at intel-lectual, emotional, physical, and spiritual compatibility—all important in making a good match.

Intellectual compatibility means being at similar levels of intellectual development. The general measure is educa-tion, but education alone does not always give a true read-ing. Compatibility means both people have comparable reasoning skills or a similar ability to study a problem or situation and come up with options but not necessarily that they think alike on every subject. It can also mean similar levels of intellectual curiosity. Some people find new ideas interesting and others find them threatening. If your differ-ences are too great, conversation becomes difficult to sus-tain, and deeper partnering is going to be a problem.

Emotional compatibility includes the degree of openness and emotional awareness each person has, which you've already seen plays a big part in the ability to build and sustain intimacy. We're all familiar with IQ tests that measure intelligence. Social scientists also talk about emotional quotient (EQ), which measures emotional capacity, potential for compassion, empathy, and ability to identify emotions and share them. You don't have to have the same feelings about everything but you must be able to accept and honor each other's emotions and feelings.

Physical compatibility refers to the potential for sexual attraction. It doesn't just mean sex appeal, which often means simply fantasizing about having sex and preferring the fantasy to actually getting to know the person. Being attracted to one another is a necessary ingredient when seeking a partner. Who appeals to you and why doesn't always make sense and doesn't need to. It's a Mother Nature thing, determined from the neck down. Healthy attraction draws two people together, sparking interest and making them want to get to know one another. However, if sex becomes the overriding consideration in selecting a date or a mate, it derails the process, and the healthy evolution of the relationship will suffer.

Spiritual compatibility describes the way you relate to life in the larger sense. It includes some of the big questions such as "Who am I?" "What is my purpose?" "What is the meaning of life?" Seekers don't seek answers from other people; they seek them from life itself. If you are a seeker, you'll find it too limiting to be with someone who has all the answers and wants to give them to you. And if you feel you already have all the answers, you'll wonder why the other person doesn't "get it." You'll find the seeker too unsettling—too out there.

Spiritual compatibility includes sharing similar values.

Values are revealed gradually over time in conversations. Pay attention to sarcastic asides followed by "just kidding." The asides may more accurately show the person's real values. In assessing values, go with what you observe rather than what a person says he values. What you see is what you get! While encountering a different value system from yours may be interesting, it generally won't make for a satisfying match in the long run. (See exercise 5 in appendix A on values clarification.)

ABLE: LIFESTYLE DIFFERENCES

Adding *able* to this discussion messes up the HOW (honest, open, and willing) acronym, but let's include it anyway. Even when all appears to line up, there can be a lifestyle difference that just won't go away, and the relationship isn't *able* to gel. This can happen, for example, when one of you is a casual, laid back, cutoff jeans kind of person and the other is highly ambitious and career focused, preferring business suits. It could also be a problem if one person loves to travel (as a lifestyle not as a hobby) and the other would rather tend the home fires. Or it could happen if one of you has young children and the other has no interest in children or can't understand why it's so difficult for you to find a sitter at the drop of a hat. Such differences can be worked through, as long as there is mutual respect for the other's style, but lifestyle differences can be difficult to resolve.

The old country song "Roll in My Sweet Baby's Arms" describes some people's idea of relationship heaven. For others togetherness is better captured in the song "Don't Fence Me In." Neither is better, and you'll find good company around either camp. The important thing is to make sure you and your partner are whistling the same tune. If you're the "lay around this shack" type and are dating a "lots of land under starry skies above" dude, there's going to be a problem.

WHEN TO HOLD 'EM AND WHEN TO FOLD 'EM

If you are looking for permanent partnering with marriage or another kind of formal arrangement, it is perfectly acceptable and appropriate to lay your cards on the table in good time—and timing is key. Typically, the right time to let your potential partner know what you're looking for in the long run would be after the initial stages of dating, as you move from dating to relating. You want to make it clear that you aren't suggesting any long-term commitment now but want to know if it is a possibility. This subject may seem like an emotional "hot potato," but think of it this way: If you're in Kansas City and want to go to New York, you don't want to catch a plane for California. Following is Lynn's experience on this very issue:

Lynn was thirty-six when she met Brad. In her words, she had endured her last round of the dating game. This time was for keeps or she was headed straight to the nunnery. Lynn and Brad first saw each other at a recovery meeting and went for coffee with the group after the meeting. A mutual friend, "Destiny," sat them together. Lynn made it clear she found Brad handsome and interesting and she was available. Brad enjoyed the flirting and asked her out. They began dating, and mutual interest continued to grow. After two months, Lynn fell apart. She began crying for no apparent reason. When Brad asked what was going on, she let out twenty years of dating frustration, concluding with "If you aren't open to the idea of marriage, you can leave right now. No explanations necessary." Brad didn't back off. He said he was definitely on board. Their dating progressed into a relationship, and they were married in six months. That was almost eleven years ago.

_____

This isn't exactly the recommended way to clarify your position, but it does show that it's all right to make your needs known.

Summary Points

- The initial phase of dating, called single and dating, stops short of emotional intimacy.
- Intimacy is the ability to recognize and share your feelings with another person. You have to be able to do that within yourself first.
- Sharing emotions is complex. It requires self-awareness, a gradual trust-building process, and skillful techniques, which all add up to commitment.
- Sharing common values is the most accurate pre-dictor of a successful relationship.

In the next chapter you'll discover the difference between meeting a soul mate and copping a love buzz. You'll read about the Healthy Relationship Pyramid and have a chance to play the Easy Does It Dating Game.

Chapter Eight *

Sex, Single, and Staying Sober

- Mother Nature's insurance policy
- Rock-my-world-*now* sex
- Three reasons why relationships fail
- Play the Easy Does It Dating Game

Nature has provided well for herself. Sex is a force to be reckoned with. This amazing drive is directly connected to our "lizard brain," the part of our mind that was wired for survival when we lived next door to the Flintstones. It contains the instinct to reproduce in order for the species to continue as well as a strong bonding force to hold a couple together. Sex, however, isn't an instinct that always has to be acted on like eating, drinking water, or sleeping. We have a choice as to when, where, and with whom we engage our sexual instinct.

This book is not suggesting any particular moral code regarding sexuality. Its purpose is to give you information and suggestions about healthy dating and relating, with the thought that an informed choice is a good one. However, what you do with this information is up to you. As is often heard in other aspects of recovery, take what works for you and leave the rest.

Nature's Laboratory: Sex, Love, and Chemistry

Throughout the ages, love and sex have been celebrated in poetry, dance, art, sacred literature, and countless bodice-ripping novels. They launched a thousand ships in the days of Troy and have spurred many a gentleman to dust off his dueling pistols and take up arms. However, what we often mistake for love and romance has more to do with lust and chemicals than heralding the arrival of a soul mate.

Under the right circumstances (such as seeing someone who matches your ideal of sexy) the brain releases phenylethylamine (PEA), dopamine, and norepinephrine, all having powerful amphetamine-like qualities. Your heart begins pounding, your mood soars, and the fantasies begin to roll. You are well on your way to a love "high." It happens whether you're a good match or get along like a mongoose and snake; in fact it doesn't matter if you even know the first name of the object of your affection. All it takes is a microscopic degree of sex appeal and a shred of emotional connection enhanced by a few candlelight dinners, and you've got pair bonding.

Pair bonding is Mother Nature's insurance policy, making certain a couple stays together and raises the kiddies. Pair bonding happens instinctively. When pair bonding happens between the wrong two people, it can create relationship hell. Once bonding sets in—regardless of whether it's a good match or a bad one—it becomes almost impossible to leave, even when violence is part of the mix. The only way to avoid stepping into those cement overshoes is conscious awareness. It's the best case there is for taking it slowly and making conscious decisions about following your dating plan rather than falling into another relationship that doesn't work from the get-go. You know the kind—misery, pain, fighting, crying, broken promises, and sometimes even broken bones.

Keep in mind that these sex chemicals are addictive. If you act on them they will behave just like any other addictive substance: your body will build a dependency and a tolerance. Even potentially great matches can fail when couples act on sexual urges before building a foundation for physical intimacy. Your addiction demands that you throw a little gasoline on the embers—increase the risk factors. It tells you to cruise the clubs, cheat on your lover, or move on. It's almost impossible for a person in early recovery to navigate this heady territory without either slipping into an old addiction or activating a new one.

It's not easy for people with lots of sobriety either, but they've got more experience to draw from. Having tasted serenity, they have a better chance of knowing when it begins slip-sliding away. Always remember, loss of serenity signals that relapse is creeping into your life.

WHO ATTRACTS US AND WHY

Chemicals called pheromones play a part in who we are attracted to and why, but they play a smaller part than was once thought. Another theory suggests we are drawn toward those who symbolize good "breeding stock" to our subconscious mind. If that were the whole case, all women would be attracted to brawny guys who can bring home the bacon and defend the nest. Yet many women find slender, fine-boned, intellectual guys their cup of tea—the ones who read the classics in the original language but can't change a flat. Likewise, male preference in mate selection runs the gamut from full-figured women, an image that has traditionally represented childbearing qualities, to the very petite.

Many psychologists believe we are attracted to certain people who resemble members of our family. We unconsciously seek them out because they symbolize the good experiences we had, or we think they will solve childhood mysteries. A man might find himself drawn to the kind of female who represents nurturing and love in a maternal way—like his mother gave him or didn't give him. She may convey this likeness through her body style or by her mannerisms. A woman may find she is attracted to a certain type of guy who says "security" to her subconscious mind. That might be financial, emotional, or physical security like her father provided—or failed to provide. You might find yourself asking, "Do we ever get past this family-of-origin stuff?" Maybe not, but we do get past its negative effects through increased awareness.

For whatever hidden reasons that lurk beneath our inner horizon, it's the physical stuff that first catches our attention—what a person looks, sounds, smells, tastes, and feels like—and this gets the game rolling. None of this has to fit the Madison Avenue ideal of beauty. We are captivated for a variety of reasons.

While physical characteristics bear responsibility for getting the love game started, other ingredients need to be stirred into the mix for the cake to rise. Physical attraction followed by a process of sharing mutual values provide the best chance at having a long-term loving relationship where serenity, happiness, and great sex abound.

WHAT'S WRONG WITH THIS PICTURE?

From Richie Cunningham and the *Happy Days* gang to *Sex and the City*, our ideas about sex have changed dramatically over the last thirty years. Despite America's pseudo-sophistication around the subject of sex, our rates of sexually transmitted diseases (STDs), teen pregnancies, and failed marriages are among the highest in the developed world. It seems we aren't looking at the whole picture.

The goal of this book is to help you learn how to date successfully. This includes three main objectives: forming a healthy relationship with yourself, making decisions about dating and relating, and staying clean and sober in either event. Jumping the gun and jumping into bed without going through the process of dating and consciously building a relationship jeopardizes all three objectives.

Most counselors agree that a primary factor in relationship failure is introducing sex into the equation too early—before emotional, intellectual, and spiritual commitments have been secured. Sex is powerful, and when it enters your relationship house before the foundation is built, the relationship often can't support it.

Here are the top three reasons relationships fail:

1. Moving too fast—meaning sex too soon
2. Being driven by the past—unresolved family-of-origin patterns
3. Making unconscious choices
   • Not knowing who you are
   • Not knowing who the other is
   • Not knowing the nature of the relationship

ROCK-MY-WORLD-*NOW* SEX

In his book *Getting Love Right*, Terence Gorski describes "blow my mind on demand" sex that characterizes addictive relationships. For our purposes here, let's borrow this concept and call it rock-my-world-*now* sex. In this kind of arrangement, a couple agrees to provide each other with sex on demand without emotional bonding or commitment. Driven by feel-good chemicals, these relationships are generally addictive and last about six months to a year. By this time the body has caught up with the chemicals, and you need an additional bounce. If this is your preferred dating and relating style, and you inform your partners up front, and you practice safe sex, *and* it still works for you, it is a personal call.

Unfortunately, rock-my-world-*now* sex often depends on raising the risk bar, eventually throwing caution to the wind, making promiscuity a predictable outcome. Most of us support the anything-goes principle between consenting adults—in theory, anyway. In reality, someone usually gets hurt—emotionally, physically, or both.

Promiscuity has negative effects. It can lead to having unprotected sex, which is like a pyramid company; you are having sex with every person that person ever had sex with and everybody that person had sex with, and so on. *Safe sex* may be an oxymoron. Maybe it should be *safer sex* because all relations with people carry risk. Safer sex means taking as much risk out of the equation as possible. The more you know about the person you're relating to the less risky it is.

Promiscuity

Promiscuity can do the following:

- Erode self-respect, dignity, and self-worth
- Reinforce your sense of worthlessness (it sends the message that you're not deserving of love)
- Make you feel disconnected
- Cause psychic numbing
- Create guilt
- Violate your own sense of values
- Increase the potential of contracting a disease

- Be potentially deadly (little preparation about basics such as birth control or condoms can be a dangerous game)
- Lead to relapse, especially in early recovery (they didn't write all those crying-in-your-beer songs for nothing)

Probably everyone has confused love with sex at some time, but they are not the same thing. There isn't one definition of love because the word *love* can mean many different things to many different people. But in general, you can think of love as an emotion beginning with attraction and feelings of romance and developing with time under the right circumstances.

Sex, on the other hand, is a biological event. And there are different kinds of sex. It may or may not include penetration. It can happen between a male and a female, between two females, between two males, or by oneself (masturbation).

Believe it or not, we make choices about sex—even about allowing ourselves to become aroused. We can turn off our sexual impulses. Making a choice about whether to allow a sexual impulse to determine your life is not sexual repression; it is a conscious decision. You can *work with* your biological impulses or allow your emotional and sexual urges to sabotage your health and happiness. Your sexuality is a matter of *your good judgment.*

Note: The words *work with* are emphasized because they match the model advocated here: finding a peaceful resolution between impulse and reason (not simply overruling one or the other). *Your good judgment* is also highlighted because judgment works best when you take responsibility for setting your boundaries rather than following a moral mandate imposed from the outside. It's a grown-up thing.

The Spirituality of Sex

We're not accustomed to hearing *sex* and *spirituality* in the same sentence. The spirituality of sex isn't about moralizing; it's about recognizing the beauty and power of sex and figuring out how to ride the wild stallion without breaking it or getting broken in the process.

Transcendence is an experience above and beyond the ordinary, and one of the ways we seek transcendence is through sex. Sex has the power to create life. That's big. It links us to God. Sex allows us the chance to let down our defenses and merge with another human being, which calls for a high level of trust—the kind that comes with time. The equation goes something like this: the more trust between partners, the more surrender, and the more surrender, the more intense the encounter. Sex can create an altered state of consciousness somewhat like the spiritual ecstasy of monks and mystics; it creates a state of serenity and bliss. These are huge dynamics when you think about it.

In a conscious relationship, intimacy builds gradually, and trust deepens. Safety allows both partners to become more vulnerable to one another—allowing deeper levels of surrender and greater pleasure. Rather than simply relying on the explosive rock-my-world-*now* chemicals, the body produces oxytocin, creating an enduring sense of calm, love, and support.

Raising Your Sensuousness Quotient, or SQ

Sensuousness describes the ability to enjoy or appreciate physical pleasure. Our pleasure receptors are developed in infancy and early childhood by physical and emotional nurturing. All that silly stuff you do with babies awakens pleasure centers in the brain—the more stimulation a new little human receives, the more the child learns to accept pleasurable sensations. When babies are held, rocked, cuddled, stroked, smiled at, cooed at, and sung to, they learn that their bodies are an enjoyable place to be and that the world is a nice place. With lots of good physical and emotional attention, the central nervous system is conditioned to feel safe and secure and comfortable, and the child learns to experience all levels of gratification.

This early development affects our ability to give and receive pleasure throughout life—influencing our ability to have satisfying sexual experiences as an adult. If you did not receive enough nurturing as an infant, your ability to feel pleasure as well as other good feelings such as comfort, security, and gratification has been compromised. You can learn to nurture and love yourself and find that calm, peaceful feeling within you—even as an adult. In recovery programs, it often begins with giving and receiving hugs.

Recovery includes learning how to take better care of yourself—to "baby" the baby that is inside you. It begins with simple things like wearing comfortable clothing, eating when you're hungry, exercising, and getting a good night's sleep.

A tried-and-true way to nurture yourself is a sensuous bath. This means bath oil, candles, soft music—the works. Creating a weekly ritual that's all about soaking in the tub, with scented oils, mud packs, sea scrubs—the whole thing—is therapeutic. Investigate herbs and teas too.

Working out at the gym followed by a steam bath, working on a home improvement project, spending a quiet evening at home, getting caught up on laundry, watching a movie or a ball game, reading, whatever is your thing, translates into loving yourself.

Gradually you awaken the sensory receptors that have

shut down and feeling good becomes the norm. Here's a quick example of how our ability to be sensitive to ourselves slowly but surely returns:

Anne was sitting on the beach talking with her sponsor. About ten minutes into their conversation, she stood up, looked at the sharp rock she was sitting on, and moved to a more comfortable place. She smiled at her sponsor and said, "Progress! Last week I would have sat on the rock an hour longer before moving."

SCRATCHING THE WRONG ITCH

Sensual deprivation starves us emotionally and drives us into a sexual relationship when what we really need is love and nurturing. Having sex because you are deprived sets you and your partner up for problems. You're scratching the wrong itch.

Feeling good physically and feeling good emotionally are interconnected, and the quickest route to emotional serenity is through the body. Many of us turned to alcohol and other drugs to fix emotional pain. In recovery, when these substances are no longer an option, sex can become a temporary substitute. Sooner or later, however, the emotional pain resurfaces. Dating and relating will have much better results when you have learned how to love and nurture yourself rather than trying to find someone to do this for you through sex. Healing begins by treating your physical body sensitively. The result is emotional security, physical comfort, and serenity. We all need each other, but each of us needs to be able to maintain a basic level of self-care. Before long, you will also realize the part of you that wants to be loved and nurtured is too young for sex; it is probably the kid inside of you.

SQ, then, can mean Serenity Quotient as well as Sensuousness Quotient. Full recovery means taking back your God-given gifts of pleasure, satisfaction, and peace—in a word—serenity.

SEXUAL INTIMACY BEGINS AT HOME

Good sex depends on being able to convey to your partner what pleasures you and what doesn't. You can't do that if you don't know. Unless you are in a recovery program that requires abstinence from all sex for a period of time, masturbation is a good way of relieving sexual tension and also a way of learning how your body works. Men seem to be way ahead of women on the matter of self-arousal and self–sexual gratification. This is a case of what's good for the gander is good for the goose.

One woman's sponsor told her she could have all the sex she wanted in her first year of recovery. In her second year she could think about including another person! It's not a bad idea for women to get a vibrator (a good one that can run a long time), name it, and build a relationship with it.

IT'S ALL IN THE TIMING

Different couples enter into sexual intimacy at different times in their relationships. Some wait until becoming engaged, and others wait until after marriage or a formal commitment ceremony. The important point to remember is that sex is very near the top of the intimacy ladder, and for the best results, it follows a time of preparation and requires a high level of commitment.

As was stated earlier, when we arrive in recovery, we're often behind on the emotional maturity curve. The point is to remain as free of the various traps surrounding addiction as possible while we finish growing up. Following is a suggested checklist to consider before moving ahead with sex in your relationship.

Pre-Sex Checklist

____ Plan your timing for sex talks. Such a discussion should happen after the third date if you both want to continue seeing each other.

____ Know what works for you. If you want to abstain from sex until engagement or marriage, let your partner know. If there is any resistance, settle it right away. If your partner doesn't agree, there will be an ongoing battle that likely will lead to you feeling hassled or compromised. You'll have to deal with this issue sooner or later.

____ Talk about what is included in becoming sexually involved.

____ Talk about what kind of commitment you need to feel safe.

____ Describe exclusivity—both physical and emotional.

____ Evaluate how sex will change the relationship.

____ Know your partner's sexual history, including any sexually transmitted diseases (previous or current), marriages, or children.

____ Schedule medical checkups, including HIV testing.

____ Discuss protection against STDs and unwanted pregnancies.

Sex Quiz

We all have many misconceptions (no pun intended) about sex—what's safe and what's not. Following are ten questions that may be helpful. The answers are found at the end of appendix A.

1. Which of the following is *not* true about having sex for the first time?

_____ a. You will never forget it.

_____ b. You don't need to use protection.

_____ c. It won't feel as good as you think it will.

_____ d. You can get pregnant or catch an STD.

2. What is the only totally effective form of birth control?

_____ a. The Pill

_____ b. Abstinence

_____ c. Condoms

_____ d. Condoms *and* the Pill

3. Which of the following is a bad reason to have sex?

_____ a. You care deeply about your partner.

_____ b. You want to share yourself with the other person.

_____ c. You are in love.

_____ d. Everyone else is doing it.

4. What type of contraception *best* protects against HIV and other STDs?

_____ a. A condom

_____ b. Two condoms used at the same time

_____ c. A diaphragm

_____ d. Withdrawal before ejaculation

5. You can best protect yourself against STDs by using a condom and spermicide.

_____ a. True

_____ b. False

6. If you are kissing or making out with somebody you *owe* the person sex if he or she wants it.

_____ a. True

_____ b. False

7. If your partner recently tested negative on an HIV test, it is safe to have sex without barrier protection.

_____ a. True

_____ b. False

8. Sex can make a bad relationship better.

_____ a. True

_____ b. False

9. (Gals) Participating in anal or oral sex doesn't count as having sex.

_____ a. True

_____ b. False

10. (Guys) It's up to her to keep from getting pregnant.

_____ a. True

_____ b. False

The Bare Minimum

Here is the *bare minimum* of information you need before making decisions about sex. It is also a good idea to educate yourself thoroughly about the risks and prevention of sexually transmitted diseases. There is good information on the Internet and at your local health department.

If you choose to have sexual intercourse, it is important to practice responsible sexual behavior. There are a number of ways you can do that, including the following:

1. Limit the number of sexual partners you have in a lifetime.
2. Avoid sexual intimacy until you and your partner have been checked for STDs.
3. Always use a latex condom and spermicide for anal and vaginal intercourse, even if one partner is using birth control pills or a diaphragm.
4. Use an unlubricated latex condom or a dental dam for oral sex. (There is risk of passing many sexually transmitted diseases from the mouth to the genital area or from the genital area to the mouth.)
5. Weigh the risk of saying no to a partner who is not willing to use condoms against the risk of exposing yourself to a life-threatening STD.
6. Know the facts: Progression of HIV/AIDS is very slow, so symptoms may not occur for years. However, a person can be contagious to others during this period. HIV attacks the body's immune system, making it difficult for a person to fight off infections. The virus that causes AIDS is not spread through the air, in food, or by casual contact such as hugging, swimming in pools, coughing, or kissing. AIDS is a fatal disease for which there is no cure.
7. Protect yourself by talking about STDs with your partner and learning as much as possible about the various types of STDs.

The Easy Does It Dating Game

The Easy Does It Dating Game was created as a way of looking at sexual intimacy in the larger context of healthy relationships. The game is based on making conscious choices as you negotiate your way through increasing levels of intimacy and commitment, as illustrated in the Healthy Relationship Pyramid that follows.

In this game, you'll look at three different approaches to the stages of dating and see which approach works best in getting to the top of the Healthy Relationship Pyramid, Easy Does It style. Only one approach will get you to the next level; however, there aren't any wrong choices, and you always have the option of selecting out at the level you can handle. Our contestant, as well as the object of his affection, might be gay or straight, young or old, male or female. Please change the pronouns to fit.

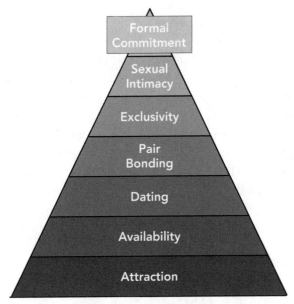

Healthy Relationship Pyramid

Back story: Let's imagine the ideal scenario. You have two years clean and sober, are working your program, and can pass the checklist found in the first chapter. You go to meetings, enjoy the fellowship, and generally know how to hang out with a degree of serenity. Under the careful eye of your sponsor, you've been dating different people for a year—keeping free and clear of emotional entanglements. You now feel the time is right to initiate the process of looking for partnership.

Level One: Attraction

Attraction begins when you are physically attracted to someone and want to know more about her.

Scene One: You're talking with friends, and someone new joins your group; you can't help but take notice. She matches your ideal, and you'd like to get to know her better. You're at level one of the Healthy Relationship Pyramid. Now let's imagine three different approaches; feel free to add yours to the game as well.

- Approach #1: You react with interest as she joins your group. You are willing to take the risk, and you begin a conversation with her.
- Approach #2: You are attracted but don't know exactly what to do next. You hold back, listen to what the others are saying, and wait to see if you can get her to make the first move.
- Approach #3: You try to listen but are preoccupied with thinking of what to say, what she will say back, and what you'll say—and ultimately you say nothing.

Level Two: Availability

Availability means neither of you are in a committed relationship, both of you are at least a year or more postdivorce, and both have a year or more of sobriety.

Scene Two: In conversation you discover that she ended a three-year relationship about a year and a half ago. Since that time she has been healing from the breakup—including working a codependency program. What do you do next?

- Approach #1: At an opportune time you ask her if she'd like to meet for coffee next week. She accepts, and you offer her your number and ask if she would like to give you hers. The night before your planned meeting, you call and confirm. Meanwhile your recovery program remains consistent.
- Approach #2: You wonder (a lot) if you should make a move but think it would be better to play it cool. You continue the conversation in your head but say nothing, coming off as not interested.
- Approach #3: You begin building a castle in the sky: your fantasy lover has the physical attributes of Jennifer Lopez, the moral fiber of Joan of Arc, and the financial empire of Oprah Winfrey. You go to meetings but leave early to go home and stare at the answering machine. You are lonely and wonder why there are never any messages.

Level Three: Dating

Dating is a time of assessment *before* bonding begins. It's not exclusive and involves no commitment.

Scene Three: Five months into dating, you both realize you really care for each other. You share many of the same values and activities; you enjoy watching foreign films and listening to jazz, and besides that, her hair smells really good. She seems to feel the same way about you. You agree that you don't want to go out with others anymore.

- Approach #1: You are happy, hopeful, and feeling lucky; you talk about gratitude at your regular meeting.
- Approach #2: You begin to worry that the relationship isn't working and start working the relationship. You feel distracted and are having trouble getting to meetings.
- Approach #3: You wonder where all this "relating" is going and think you'd both be better off with less talk and more sex. You're going to meetings but are isolating—not telling anyone what's really going on inside.

Level Four: Pair Bonding

Pair bonding is the physical and emotional attachment that naturally happens when you spend time with a person and are connecting emotionally.

Scene Four: Conversation deepens and emotional bonding sets it. You've met each other's friends, and all is going well. You look into each other's eyes and talk about being together forever. You both would like to have sex but are talking about the possible risks, weighing them against the benefits. You realize this is the time for full disclosure and talk about each other's past—even that rainy night in Georgia. You feel safe. You've had a couple of arguments and have worked through them.

- Approach #1: You're feeling good about life; you're still sober and going to meetings and have successfully applied program principles to your disagreements. You're entering new emotional territory, discovering feelings you didn't know you had—feeling excited and scared at the same time.

- Approach #2: You're feeling fearful and trapped; you become obsessive about the relationship, begin shutting down, and only go to meetings when the pain is really bad. You wonder why it always turns out like this.
- Approach #3: You are sensing that things are going well and can sniff commitment in the wind. You promptly terminate the relationship, wondering why it always turns out like this.

Level Five: Exclusivity

Exclusivity is a time of clarifying your commitment, making mutual decisions about becoming sexual, and making preparations if that is what is decided.

Scene Five: It's been a year since the two of you met, and on your anniversary you announce your intentions to be together. You decide the time is right to begin sexual intimacy. You get medical checkups, which include having HIV tests and inquiring about birth control, and are planning your first night together. You want just the right touch of romance without overdoing it and looking goofy.

- Approach #1: You are nervous and excited. You go out to dinner with your sponsor and go home feeling comfortable. Acting on your sponsor's advice, you pray for guidance and courage. You vow to take it one day at a time and leave the results to your Higher Power.
- Approach #2: You totally freak. You feel out of control and can't breathe. You think your partner is

rushing things. You want to put the commitment issue on hold and stop answering the phone when she calls. Your relationship breaks up, and you enter a relapse cycle.

- Approach #3: You are long gone.

Level Six: Sexual Intimacy

Sexual intimacy often begins at this level; however, some couples decide to wait until after the formal commitment, which is at the top of the pyramid.

Scene Six: You are in love with each other. You are talking about the benefits and pitfalls of moving in together—wondering if it's what you both want. You decide on how to honor your relationship by finding a way each of your needs can be met. You're planning a commitment ceremony and deciding if marriage will follow.

- Approach #1: Sometimes you feel scared but know you're doing the right thing. You meet with your sponsor regularly and are discovering more about yourself every day. You are going to regular meetings and still emotionally taking it one day at a time.
- Approach #2: You realize you are in over your head and get back to working your program and hanging out with friends. You feel better.
- Approach #3: You are "over it" and are interested in someone new.

Level Seven: Formal Commitment

Formal commitment includes deepening levels of intimacy, which may include marriage, a commitment ceremony with family and friends, or a statement made between the couple.

Scene Seven: This step has taken you to the top of the pyramid clean and sober and shouting hallelujah! You have grown in your spiritual life and gained insight. You realize there are good times and difficult times in this relationship and still want to proceed. You make a mutual decision with your partner to get couple's counseling and are generally looking forward to life. You continue going to meetings and are comfortable in your recovery.

In this game the first approach in each of the levels is the ideal. Don't be discouraged if it felt too hard or just plain odd. Recovery means progress not perfection. It often takes more than one attempt when doing something new. Like the other approaches showed us, everyone deserves the right to make choices; we learn new things when we're ready. Remember: Always do what you need to do to take care of yourself.

SUMMARY POINTS

- A slow and conscious approach to dating and relating provides the best chance of success.
- Physical attraction is a powerful force that will turn your relationship into concrete fairly quickly.
- The concrete sets whether it's a good relationship or a bad one.
- Entering into sexual intimacy before the emotional, intellectual, and spiritual foundation is built usually results in the collapse of a relationship.
- Taking responsibility for your sexuality includes making decisions about who, where, what, why, and when.

The same basic approach applies to everyone who is dating. However, the next chapter will cover some of the particular challenges, such as dating others in recovery, same-sex dating, dating when children are part of the arrangement, and dating among the over-sixty crowd.

Chapter Nine *

Variations on a Theme

- Considerations in "fellowship" dating.
- Is it normal for kids to jump on the couch and scream "I hate you" when you bring a date home?
- Is it okay to send the kids to summer camp in January?
- How AA got the Third Tradition.
- Will you still love me when you're sixty-four?

The principles of recovery have been time-tested and found to apply to people from all walks of life and all circumstances. In fact, nowhere in our culture will you find a better example of variety being the spice of life than in the recovering community. The *Easy Does It Dating Guide* applies these principles to a dating plan that can be helpful in all situations. This chapter explores several variations on a theme, examining factors unique to particular lifestyles as well as looking at how dating follows essentially the same process regardless of lifestyle.

RECOVERING COUPLES: TO BE OR NOT TO BE

There are advantages and disadvantages to dating others in recovery. Relationships and marriages between recovering couples enjoy about the same success rate as any other group of people. Certainly the probability of meeting someone at a

Twelve Step meeting with values similar to yours is high. Working the same spiritual program and dealing with similar concerns brings a deep sense of connection; you both speak the same language and share a common approach to problem solving. You could be each other's support system, encouraging each other.

On the other hand, the chances of meeting people with experiences and worldviews very different from yours is every bit as high as meeting kindred spirits. In addition, sharing recovery means both of you will be dealing with similar challenges—and the probability of hitting the same walls at the same time doubles. When it comes to choosing partnership from the recovering community, you should use the same process as when selecting from the larger community. Both situations require a cautious examination of compatibility. In brief: Carrying matching anniversary coins doesn't necessarily ensure you are both carrying matching values.

What about Meetings?

If you do date someone from your meeting, you'll need to consider a few issues. One plan doesn't fit all when it comes to how recovering couples handle their meeting schedules, as the following stories show. Most have found it helpful to add an Al-Anon or a CoDA meeting to their schedule, and most couples prefer to share a meeting and keep at least one to themselves. The important thing is to stay with your program—getting to enough meetings, enjoying the fellowship, and adding meetings to your schedule if you need more support. Success depends on each person following a recovery program, staying aware of the disease, and recognizing when one or the other is in trouble.

Ben and Sally attended the same meeting for several years before they began dating. They've been seeing each other for a year and consider the meeting where they met as "theirs." In addition, Ben goes to his men's meeting and Sally goes to her women's meeting. Their relationship is moving toward a stronger commitment. However, if it doesn't work out, they decided that they would deal with who gets the shared meeting and who gets the cat at the same time.

———————

Michael and Louis had been attending the same men's meeting for several years. When they broke up, they tried to keep the meeting separate from the relationship but couldn't make that work. According to Michael, "It was just too hard to see Lou and hear him talk at meetings. We had such different versions of what went wrong. I got mad if he didn't say anything about the relationship and mad if he did. I found it worked better for me to find a different meeting. Maybe someday I'll be ready to be in the same meeting with Lou, but not today."

———————

Weathering the Storms in a Clean-and-Sober Relationship

Even when all the bases are covered, there aren't any guarantees in life or in recovery. The disease of addiction includes relapse. Solid recovery and knowledge of the disease can help couples recognize and flag a relapse cycle in the early stages and offer help to each other. If a full-blown relapse occurs in one or both partners, as in the story that follows, having a program to rely on can make a huge difference in weathering bad times.

———————

Jan and Frank were old friends and ran into each other at a meeting a few months after each of them had ended a relationship. They began dating and six months later decided to date each other exclusively. They've been together for seven years.

Three years into the relationship Frank relapsed. Jan added Al-Anon to her life and was able to hang in for a year, but the desire to fix Frank drove her into relapse. They drank together for the next two years. Jan said she continued going to meetings, praying, and doing what she was taught to do, but the drinking continued. A year later a combination of physical problems and emotional pain brought Frank back into recovery. He stepped up his meetings, adding men's Al-Anon, and was able to get enough detachment to hang in there while Jan continued drinking for another year.

Jan got back into recovery with the help of a therapist. Now they attend two meetings together each week. Despite their relapses, Jan believes their relationship is stronger because of the program. She feels it's better for her to be with another alcoholic because recovery gives them common ground rules for handling life and disagreements that go with living. Jan says that they often go through all their "stuff" before finally getting to the "principles before personalities" part, but at least they finally get there.

Sharing Program Wisdom

Even if you don't date someone who is in the program, you can still make program wisdom a part of your relationship together. See the following story as an example:

Tracy has five years in recovery from drug addiction. She is dating Montiel who does not have the disease of addiction. Tracy finds it refreshing to be with someone who isn't facing the same recovery challenges she faces. At the same time, however, they are both in graduate school and have many of the same problems—essentially how to fit two day's activities into each day, all week long. Tracy says it is a complete surprise to her to see how differently they go about dealing with life. She uses program principles to handle her stress. "Montiel has many of the same principles; they seem to be built into his system," she says. "However, every now and then, he is up against something he can't get a handle on, and I am able to offer a program tidbit such as 'Just take it one day at a time, Montiel.' He is amazed at my wisdom. He particularly loves the one about if I didn't break it I don't have to fix it. Someday he'll probably go to some meeting and find out I didn't personally invent these sayings."

When Kids Are Part of the Equation

Dating when children are part of the equation adds complexity, to say the least. The particulars of how to handle your situation depend on the age of the children involved, how long you've been a single parent, and how well everyone is adjusting. In the case of divorce, factors such as the amount of shared parenting, special needs or considerations, as well as the quality of child care come into play. This discussion can only touch on the basics, and it is advisable to get additional information from one of the many books on the subject of single parenting.

Whether you are a divorced parent, have lost a spouse to death, or have never married, the first thing to consider is that life goes on: You have a right to begin dating again. Let's assume you have gone through the first stages of grieving and that you've spent a year or more recovering from the breakup. When you have children and are dating, you'll need to consider two main points: your need for privacy and your children's right to security and to know what's happening. Both are important, and it takes considerable presence, awareness, and skill to manage those dynamics.

Following are some basic guidelines when dealing with kids and dating:

- Be clear in your mind that you are dating for you, not for the children's sake, and that it is natural and appropriate to want this in your life.
- At the same time, if you are seeking partnership, consider the relationships between your potential partner and the children as a factor.
- Don't rush to fill the emptiness you are feeling. You are a family—a bonded group. Give everyone time to adjust as you go. This is the same advice for singles without kids. Go slowly! Go twice as slow when kids are involved.
- Be honest! Sometimes the kids get in the way. It's better to deal with the complications you're facing up front—with a sponsor or counselor—than to let them sneak up on you. If you are feeling the burden but aren't letting on at home, it gets weird for the kids. They sense your frustration and think they're doing something wrong.
- Work on exhibiting your maturity, patience, honesty, and love. Even then, it's going to be hard at times, and there isn't any way to avoid some of the complications you'll be facing. Everyone— including you—will make mistakes. Words like *patience*, *compromise*, and *forgiveness* will take on new meanings.
- Know that it's normal to feel some guilt about dating—but don't wallow in it. There's been a loss in your life and in the lives of your children. You can't make up the difference by taking on all the

responsibility. Be sensitive to everyone's emotional needs, including yours. When it's time, you need to go on with your life. The kids count on you to show them how life works. It gives them permission to go on with theirs too. Eventually, through consistency, attention, and information, everyone grows.

Kids and Early Stages of Dating

In the early stages of dating, it's recommended that you let your children know you are meeting new people and beginning to date. That's enough information for now. Let them know you're going to dinner with a friend, when you'll be home, and how to reach you. Keep it light and natural. Avoid bringing your date to the house to meet your kids. Bringing too many new people into their lives is upsetting. Save the introductions for when you make the choice to develop a more committed relationship.

Kids have built-in radar exceeding NASA standards. In fact, NASA could take lessons from them. If you don't tell them you're dating, they pick it up in your tone of voice, your attitude as you prepare to go out, or in a million other ways we can only imagine, and then they get worried or concerned.

Most kids will essentially see your dates as threats to their security—at least in the beginning. When the time comes and you bring someone home to meet your children, expect the worst. Or at least don't be surprised to find them jumping on the couch, bouncing the cat, or doubled over with a bellyache. This, of course, depends on their ages. Sometimes older kids go out looking for a date for you. Kids will express their stress in a variety of creative ways. They're just doing their job. It's up to you to stay cool and understand what's going on.

As your relationship develops and if you and your

partner become sexual, you'll probably want more guidelines than this book offers to handle the increased complexity. See appendix B for books on this and other topics; you may also wish to work with a counselor if it begins to feel unmanageable. When it gets tough, remember you are doing the best you can. You're staying clean and sober, becoming a better parent, and continuing to develop your life. In the long run, the kids will pick up on the lessons you're transmitting through your responsibility.

Following is the story of Demitra as she resumes dating as a single mom. It takes a little time, but she does eventually "get her groove back."

It took Demitra five years after her divorce to begin dating. She said time was the biggest factor; she didn't have any to spare. She was a single mom managing work, three kids, and sobriety. "By the time I got home from work, fixed supper, helped the kids with their homework and everything else, the only thing I wanted to do was crawl into bed—alone!

"I was lucky to get to my two meetings on the weekend. My sponsor is actually the one who brought up the topic of dating. She said it was time for me to move on in my life and that having some fun on dates was next in my recovery program. I was not so sure. The first time I went out, the sitter called to say my son had cut his head and needed to go to the emergency room. My date took me home immediately. It was only a small cut, and I was able to hold it together with a butterfly bandage.

"When I called my date to give him the good news, he said he thought we better hold off for a while. My sponsor wouldn't let me quit. I eventually found out that the kids would learn to accept the fact that I was dating, and I had to accept the fact that they'd keep on doing what kids do—fall down, get hurt, and live through it.

"It hasn't been easy, but I have gradually learned to enjoy myself again in recovery. The kids have learned to do their laundry, and we all pitch in on Saturday to give the house a good cleaning. To tell the truth, I'm happier than I've ever been, and you know what they say, 'If mama's happy, everybody's happy!'"

Dating when you both have kids can be stressful to each of you and to the relationship, so can dating someone who has children when you don't. And there are also the challenges and stressors that go with blending families. Program principles give guidelines for successful interactions in all situations. Making sure you have lots of program support is vital, working with a family counselor is strongly recommended, and a trip to the library or local bookstore to check out additional resources on the topic is a good idea. While the stress factors have dominated the discussion, there is also a lot of joy in creating a new family. If it seems that you aren't making headway in that direction, consider getting more help.

"THE ONLY REQUIREMENT . . ."

The only requirement for membership in Alcoholics Anonymous and all other Twelve Step Programs is the desire to stop drinking (or stop whatever addiction your program addresses). Did you know that this requirement was the result of a debate in Dr. Bob's Akron group regarding admitting homosexuals—delicately described at the time as "a man with another problem"? The discussion began in 1945 when Bill Wilson saw that gay and bisexual men in AA had more trouble maintaining their sobriety than heterosexual men.

As a result of that discussion, the rights of people of all cultures, as well as gay, lesbian, or bisexual people, to attend any and all Twelve Step meetings was secured in the Third of the Twelve Traditions. In addition to regular meetings, there are gay and lesbian meetings, group activities, club-houses, and weekend roundups.

Ozzie and Ozzie—Harriet and Harriet

Criteria for same-sex dating and forming partnerships are no different than the criteria laid out for hetero couples, and at the same time there are additional complications for those pursuing same-sex relationships.

Honesty in meetings can include the need to talk about oneself as a gay, lesbian, or bisexual person. This can mean a forced outing and can expose a person to any homophobic re-actions that might be in the room. Many segments of society haven't separated sexual orientation from morality. Not shar-ing means holding part of your story back and can create the feeling of hiding out or less-than-rigorous honesty. To share openly about sexuality presents the risk of hearing "Take it to a gay meeting." If gay people are relegated to "their own" meetings, they are marginalized, and the program's spirit of unity is compromised; the fellowship is weakened.

Most everyone agrees that same-sex meetings are valu-able in recovery. Men and women have different experi-ences, some of which are better addressed in meetings of like gender. For example, gender-specific meetings prevent refer-ences to sex from being misunderstood. However, when you apply the same premise to gay and lesbian people, the dy-namics change significantly. The question exists in the minds of some: Is a gay man at a men's meeting for the same pur-pose as the other men? Ed's story, which follows, is a good example of this dynamic:

———————

Ed is gay and goes to a weekly men's meeting in addition to a mixed meeting. In the past he attended a gay men's meeting but didn't find the necessary support there. "Most of my issues are about my drug addiction, not my sexual orientation," Ed says. "I want to go where I can find the most recovery, and most of the time that's in the regular men's meeting. However, there are a few guys there who have problems with homosexuals. I made the mistake of asking one to be my sponsor, not knowing the situation. He told me to find a gay sponsor. Since then I have been self-conscious about sharing. I am always second-guessing myself to make sure I'm not isolating if I don't talk, and I'm also aware of my tendency to want to share 'at' him. I'm working through it with my sponsor—a straight guy—but it's been awkward at times."

Denise, on the other hand, found that most things worked out for her at meetings:

Denise attends both gay and straight women's meetings and also mixed-gender meetings, feeling comfortable and welcome in all of them. Her experience has been that the recovering community is more open and nonjudgmental than any other group of people she knows. "I don't differentiate between gay and straight. I don't care about a person's sexual orientation, and I don't believe my friends do either," Denise says. "I care about staying clean and sober and being of service to others who want a clean-and-sober way of life. Later, when I decide to start dating, I trust things will work out; that is the main thing I've learned in recovery. Most things work out."

Where to Go: A Limited Field

Theoretically, gay, lesbian, and bisexual people are as welcome as heterosexual people in the social circles listed in chapter 6. In reality this may not be true. Homophobia remains a fact of life, presenting an additional challenge to integrating into society, which is daunting enough for anyone in recovery. Once this hurdle has been crossed, there is the matter of percentages; the likelihood of meeting other gay people at these places is not very high.

For a variety of reasons, the gay community traditionally gathers in gay bars or clubs where alcohol is served, making meeting other clean-and-sober gay people who are interested in healthy dating and forming lasting relationships more challenging. Here is a chapter in Todd's story:

Todd talks about the difficulty he has in meeting other gay men in recovery. He has lots of friends among the men in his home group, as well as others in recovery, but he misses the gay community he lived in when he was using.

The first time he got sober, he returned to his former lover and continued their social life, much of which took place in bars and in private homes. Both environments relied heavily on alcohol and other drug use. Todd relapsed fairly quickly and re-entered recovery in six months after attending a treatment facility. He now has almost two years clean time and has stayed out of relationships and clubs. In his words, "I have to rebuild almost my entire life. In the world I came from, sex was the accepted way of life. Sure, there was a growing price we paid in risk, but most of us used safe sex. The point is, not many were all that wrapped up in exclusivity. Commitment, yes, but exclusivity, no. Commitment was often financial and emotional—like a social insurance policy—but physically it wasn't given much weight. Couples who respected one another didn't flaunt their affairs, but both knew about them.

"I don't know where to begin looking for someone to date. It's the same with a lot of the other guys too. The recovering gay community is really small, and I have my doubts about dating in that environment. Actually I have my doubts about dating someone in recovery, I mean, someone with this disease. It seems there is enough to deal with in relationships without all the trauma-drama that's typical of addicts—even recovering ones."

Different Sexual Mores

Many gay relationships follow different cultural mores than those in the hetero culture. At least half of gay male relationships are open, without the same emphasis on commitment or exclusivity as hetero relationships. The prevalence of HIV and AIDS in the gay male culture presents additional complications to dating and relating. Many come into recovery grieving the loss of friends who succumbed to AIDS and are dealing with their own survivor guilt.

As was mentioned earlier, childhood dynamics establish relationship patterns in adult life. In gay and lesbian relationships, there are additional factors to consider. Women's nurturing nature is both a product of hormones and role modeling. Two females in a same-sex relationship can make boundary-setting more difficult and increase the likelihood of codependency. Similarly, two men are apt to have an abundance of male qualities, such as independence and competition, and be short on nurturing skills. Whether these are bona fide male and female qualities or the result of socialization doesn't matter.

In recovery, gay and lesbian couples have greater difficulty in finding healthy role models for relationships than hetero couples do. Sheer percentages play a part as well as the lack of an established couples community—either in recovery or outside of it. Finding sponsorship as well as additional counseling is more difficult. Resources for further reading are included in appendix B in the back of the book.

OVER SIXTY BUT NOT OVER THE HILL

Dating and relating for seniors follows the same basic plan outlined in this book with a couple of additional considerations. By this time in life, your circle probably includes long-time friends and family members, including grown children and grandchildren, which can translate into more opinions and more people who need to be satisfied. However, on the other side of things, a person of maturity has most likely worked through identity issues, childhood stuff, and pretty much knows what will work and what won't when it comes to relating. As long as established preferences don't add up to inflexibility, life experience can be a decided advantage.

Seniors who are new to recovery, those recovering from divorce or death of a spouse, and those who are alone for any other reason can find themselves up against challenges that many of their contemporaries aren't facing. Starting over at a time in your life when others your age are settling in can be daunting. Isolation and loneliness can have a sharper edge during later years than earlier in life. New relationships can bring complications at any age. This can be particularly true when each person brings years of accumulation to a new partnership. As was mentioned earlier, children (including adult children) and grandchildren need to be considered. Sometimes there are issues with former spouses, in-laws, businesses, and property to be dealt with too. However, there is also a good supply of wisdom to draw on. Mattie and Ben's story shows how they handled many of these challenges:

Mattie and Ben were both in their early sixties when they met at a fund-raiser for the local animal shelter. Ben is in Twelve Step recovery, working programs for alcoholism, gambling, and codependency. His sponsor suggested he help at the shelter as a way of contributing to the community. His marriage ended in divorce two years before, which propelled him into recovery. Mattie, divorced ten years, has spent much of her time and energy developing her landscaping business. She volunteers at the animal shelter on weekends. Mattie was married to an alcoholic for many years.

Mattie and Ben were immediately drawn to each other, and after two weekends of working together, Ben asked Mattie to join him for a casual dinner after work. They had a good time and began making it a regular occasion—finding small, inexpensive restaurants for early Saturday night dinners. When Ben told Mattie he was in recovery, she stiffened. Having experienced many years of her former husband's alcoholism, she was reluctant, fearing a repetition of the past. Ben felt her discomfort, and his disappointment was overwhelming. His sponsor suggested being candid with Mattie. He advised Ben to share his feelings and discuss her fears about addiction. If she agreed, they could check out an Al-Anon meeting together.

They began attending the meeting regularly, talking afterward about their experiences—her marriage with an alcoholic and Ben's regrets at making a mess out of his marriage. Mattie was honest about the fear of losing herself again. She didn't want to take attention away from her work, which she loved as it was an art as well as a livelihood. Trust between them built gradually. Mattie liked Ben a lot but knew she needed to set her boundaries and be able to hold the line. Ben knew he needed to stay focused on recovery and to see his relationship with Mattie less as a chance to make up for his failed marriage and more as a completely new experience with a new person.

They both agreed that partnering at this time in life was different than the first time around. They had a stronger sense of who they were and what they wanted from a partnership. Their experience helped them realize that their friendship and relationship was better than average. They agreed on the big issues. The "problems" were more imagined than real—coming from the fear that things wouldn't work out, not that they weren't working out. The wisdom of experience plus recovery principles made it easier to look at the relationship with some objectivity and to appreciate the good things they could offer one another. They decided to make the saying "take what you like and leave the rest" their temporary vision statement. It kept them both focused on what worked between them and gave them the impetus to ignore the small differences.

Today they are committed to each other and to recovery. There have been a lot of family considerations to work through, and they have finally decided on marriage. They have structured their relationship on the program framework—and like to point out that they took the Twelfth Step literally where it says "[P]ractice these principles in all our affairs."

Summary Points

- Principles of Easy Does It Dating are based on program principles and apply to recovering people in all situations.
- Following a time of grieving from divorce or the death of a spouse, it's normal and healthy to date again.

- Children can be upset when you date, but in the long run, it lets them know it's all right to go on with life.
- Recovering individuals in gay and lesbian relationships encounter the same challenges as hetero relationships, with some additional considerations.
- Using program principles to help sort out the past from the present gives second tries a better chance. It's never too late to have a happy relationship.

Sometimes, despite our best efforts, a relationship doesn't make it. In the next chapter you'll find some suggestions that can help you recognize when it's over and things you can do to take care of yourself when it ends.

Chapter Ten *

Breaking Up: Damage Control

- When the head and heart disagree.
- Can you let go without leaving claw marks?
- When to move on and when to dig in.
- Pain is normal; suffering is optional.

Making conscious choices and using a step-by-step approach to dating improves your odds for having a successful relationship, but life holds no guarantees. Sometimes, despite our best efforts, love doesn't bloom. Whether to stay or whether to go is seldom an easy choice, and if pair bonding has happened, it's an even harder one. You've invested considerable time and emotional energy into the relationship. You have your personal hopes and dreams to consider and those you and your partner created together—or thought you did.

Being in the cross fire between what you think you ought to do and what your emotions want you to do is never comfortable. It's that same conversation between head and heart mentioned earlier. The dilemma resolves when you listen to both. This means if you feel the feelings and talk things through with sponsors and friends, you'll eventually find peace. The art lies in finding the balance point as you go through the process. In your heart, you want to be able to feel and release your emotions, but you don't want to be overcome by them or act on them inappropriately. In your head, you want to be able to make sense out of your experience, but overanalyzing gets you nowhere.

The bottom line is that you're hurting, either because one of you has decided to end the relationship or because you know a breakup is inevitable.

READING THE WATER

It would be great if you could know whether your love boat is sinking or just needs to be bailed. Given your history and that of your partner, it can be difficult to know whether a pattern from the past is telling you to jump ship prematurely or to stay on board and ride it to the bottom of the sea. No external criteria can be counted on absolutely, but there are definite indicators that tell you when your relationship is headed for the rocks.

Running into the same challenges over and over again, such as always partnering with someone who can't or won't commit, is one sign of trouble, but it doesn't necessarily mean it's time to lower the lifeboat. In fact, identifying the pattern offers you an opportunity to resolve your core issues. Patterns from childhood emerge in intimate relationships and require attention and healing. Usually if one person is running into her childhood stuff, the other one is too, and the patterns are getting built into the relationship. Both partners need to be on board to find resolution. If either one isn't willing or able to participate in problem solving, there is no reason to expect things will suddenly change. Recovery has taught you to look at what is, not what might be.

On another level, you could be mismatched in your capacity for intimacy or willingness to commit. Signs of incompatibility may have surfaced earlier, but you might not have read them exactly right or may have made excuses for them—another case of progress not perfection. And some things are only revealed through time. For example, you both might say you're ready for commitment but later discover that your partner's idea of commitment includes spending every Sunday at his mother's house and yours is to spend the day in bed reading the *New York Times* together.

Passing the Buck

When intimacy or commitment doesn't line up, we sense it and smell change in the wind. Anticipating change often brings fear. Remember the formula for emotions: feel them, name them, interpret them, and act appropriately. When we haven't put words on our fear, we act it out—inappropriately. It's not unusual for one partner to use acting-out behavior in an attempt to force the other person to leave. Examples of such behaviors include the following:

- Being emotionally, mentally, or physically abusive
- Creating distance by withholding communication, time, or expressions of love
- Failing to keep promises, such as sexual exclusivity
- Acting chronically discontent and finding fault constantly—the list of problems just keeps getting longer
- Withholding affection—the day-to-day smiles or hugs that keep people together
- Constantly arguing over meaningless things
- No longer talking about future plans
- Not returning each other's calls

WHEN IT'S OVER

Relationships have a shelf life; when they're over, they're over. When you recognize the end is inevitable, you have essentially three choices. You can stay, you can take time out from the relationship, or you can leave. All three choices require change; you, your partner, and the relationship will change—and that is difficult. Ideally the decisions are made together and sometimes with the benefit of a third party to help sort through the particulars.

When one person holds on despite the declining conditions, it's usually out of fear. The truth is that if one partner is having so much difficulty that she is considering ending the relationship, the other one is likely having problems as well. Few relationships can sustain that much dissatisfaction; it takes a lot of rowing to get across the river. Following are common but not good enough reasons people stay when the signs are saying it's over:

- Being afraid of loneliness or wanting to avoid other emotional pain
- Not wanting to hurt the other's feelings
- Doubting perceptions (for example, *I'm not really feeling what I'm feeling* or *I must be wrong*)
- Attempting to rationalize your experience away
- Not wanting to "waste" the time and energy already invested
- Not wanting anyone else to "get" your partner

If you make the decision to stay, regardless of the conditions, make certain you can live with the situation exactly as it is. In truth, staying when things aren't working will often mean settling for less than you had hoped for and will likely create anger and resentment down the road.

Eventually, if you've settled into a long-term relationship

such as marriage, these guidelines take on a different twist. There are often particular reasons for staying that override your desire to leave. Strong religious or spiritual convictions, children to raise, or other family expectations may require maintaining the family unit. In these cases it may be important to weather the storm, all the while staying aware of what's happening, making sure you're talking with your sponsor, and handing it over to your Higher Power. It's possible things will improve dramatically, or you'll get the spiritual insight you need to make peace with your circumstances.

When and Why to Call Time-Out

Taking time out of a relationship can be a good idea to allow either or both parties a chance to cool off or get in touch with feelings. A time-out is different than a marital separation before divorce. It's done with the intention of getting back together. A time-out brings clarity to the situation and provides a chance to re-evaluate the relationship and the problems. A time-out needs clear boundaries—rules that both agree to go by. For example, it is best when the couple agrees to a mutually beneficial time limit—whether it be a week, a month, or longer. Identify specific points of conflict that each of you wants to clarify for yourself during this period. Other considerations include establishing ground rules about seeing others, setting up times to check in with each other, and deciding how emergencies will be handled.

Problem-Solving Techniques

Often in the past you have either cut and run or put on your helmet, hunkered down, and stayed. Neither of these extreme reactions to problems are creative solutions. Both are coping behaviors. If you decide on a time-out following an initial cooling-off time, you might want to follow this problem-solving process used by mediators:

1. Identify the problem. Become as clear as you can about the attitude or behavior that is causing this problem. Sound it out with a friend, but don't air personal matters indiscriminately. Discuss matters with your sponsor or talk with a counselor.
2. Experience the emotions that you're having regarding the situation with the help of a good friend or your sponsor.
3. Decide what you need out of the situation. What changes or different behavior would you accept?
4. Make an appointment to talk with your partner, indicating the relative seriousness of what concerns you.
5. Explain your situation, saying how it makes you feel *without* getting all the feelings up and running.
6. Be willing to listen to the other side of the situation, that is, get your partner's reactions.
7. Determine if you are both willing to participate in finding a solution.
8. Brainstorm possible solutions, without criticizing or editing at this time. After brainstorming, go through the solutions and find out which ones are possible for both of you to accept. Decide on a process for implementing the new behavior.
9. Set up a trial time and a time to get back together and re-evaluate.
10. Attempt to agree on what needs to happen next using input from both of you.

If agreement can't be found using this process, it's most likely time to begin closure.

Completing a Relationship

Sometimes we don't give the other person enough credit or the benefit of the doubt. If you are unhappy and the other person can't do anything about it, there's a good chance she would be willing to end the relationship. Most of us don't want to take prisoners.

Ending a relationship is best accomplished the same way you got into the relationship—by using a conscious process. Most of us don't want to create more jagged edges or leave claw marks. Usually we just want out. The goal is to end things as gracefully as possible. That means no surprises. It's not all right to suddenly announce to your partner that it's over. Dating, relating, committing, and breaking up are all *processes*. The following sections contain advice on how to carry out the breaking-up process.

1. Avoid the Blame Game

Spending time and energy on who is right or wrong is damaging to both of you. It creates more bad feelings that generally don't get resolved. Your intention is to bring this relationship to the most peaceful completion possible, so don't dredge up more stuff. When you do, it's usually to convince yourself that you're right.

2. Get to the Emotions of the Situation

You care about one another or you wouldn't have gotten this far. Identify your feelings and be willing to experience them. This helps you avoid moralizing, which is just a way of staying out of the emotions. If you are fearless in facing your feelings, you will eventually find a place of resolution. Call it grace, forgiveness, or just plain love; something inside will shift.

3. Take Responsibility for Your Stuff

The end of a relationship can leave you feeling powerless—particularly if you aren't the one initiating the breakup. Taking responsibility for your part in it involves your adult mind and gives you a sense of your power. (It's the child part of you that feels victimized and the parent part that wants to "protect" you by making the other person wrong.) Keep reminding yourself that you're powerless over your partner's actions but not over yours; that's the grown-up speaking.

Ask yourself the following questions:

- How did I get this far in the relationship?
- Was I truly blindsided?
- Was I ignoring the problems?
- Did I think I could handle more than I could?
- Did I discover that I wasn't ready for this level of intimacy?
- Go back over your Fourth Step and identify former patterns. Ask yourself, "Have I stepped back into the past?"

4. Count the Blessings

No relationship is all bad or all good. Identify the things you value—what you wouldn't change or wouldn't want to change in the other person or the relationship. It's always "both/and"; there are *both* positive *and* negative parts to your experience. We don't grow and learn when we're trying to make it all one way.

5. Separate before Leaving

Depending on the length of time and the depth of the relationship, you both may need a period of time in which to assess positions and deal with feelings. Stay emotionally available to your partner while he goes through this initial grieving if at all possible. If your talks cross the line and become abusive, suspend them for now with the possibility of continuing later. Ask your sponsors to help.

6. Establish a Time and Place for Meeting

Have your talk on neutral ground—not at either of your homes. This can feel odd when you've been close, but it lets you both realize things are different. It also helps keep you from falling back into the relationship (or back in bed) out of habit or familiarity.

7. Let Go of Your Fantasy

If you've made up your mind to end the relationship, it's better to let the other person know this rather than implying that things might work out later. If you are the one hearing what you don't want to hear, take matters slow and avoid reshaping the circumstances in your mind. In other words, accept what is happening.

8. Make a Clear Break

Chances are you can't be friends right now—maybe not ever—so steer away from the let's-be-friends trap. Let the relationship go. If something is supposed to happen, it will, but don't try to will it into happening.

9. Apologize for Any Wrongdoing (Tenth Step)

A vague apology never works. Identify your part in any wrongdoing and apologize specifically. For example, "I'm sorry I was dishonest about the things that weren't working for me. I was afraid of hurting you, and now I have hurt you even more than if I had been honest."

10. Be Honest and Respectful

You have the right to end your relationship—and the responsibility to do it respectfully. It's not uncommon for there to be tears, anger, and promises to change. Be sensitive and stay the course. If you are supposed to be together, you will come back together. If you're not, nothing can keep the relationship together. Backtracking only delays the inevitable.

11. Examine Childhood Issues

If you are experiencing an extremely difficult time during your breakup, and it doesn't match the facts, meaning the intensity of your feelings is disproportionate to the reality of the relationship, the breakup is probably triggering childhood issues as it is with Tyler in the following example:

Tyler knew for some time that his relationship wasn't working. As he talked about it with friends, he became aware that he and his partner weren't matched in many significant ways. At one point he even realized he had not liked Lynne to begin with. He remembered that he couldn't seem to help himself as he slid deeper and deeper into it, ignoring the information and his feelings. Yet when they began to break up, he became inconsolable.

"I thought I was going to die," he said. "It hurt so bad I would have done anything to keep it going. Luckily, Lynne was adamant, saying nothing I could do would fix it. She was also honest, saying it wasn't me, that it was the relationship; it just wasn't right. As much as I hated it and because I simply couldn't avoid it, we broke up. On the suggestion of my home group, I began attending Adult Children of Alcoholics [ACA] meetings. It was the right solution. I was locked in the throws of childhood stuff. I stayed with the process for a year and a half, hurting almost every day. I learned a lot about myself, and I learned I don't want to repeat that experience. I'm dating again now and talk about taking things slowly. We are creeping through this one. I check in with my ACA group and sponsor regularly. I know I need all the help I can get."

WHEN THE STAKES ARE HIGH

"Prenuptial freak out" is normal—the higher the stakes the greater the impact on emotion. There is a difference between feeling nervous or frightened when approaching significant life events—marriage being high on the list of significant events—and indications we are making a mistake.

When the time comes to set the date and plan the ceremony, many couples include prenuptial counseling. They are dealing with not only all the feelings that go with commitment but also the thousand and one decisions to be made regarding the ceremony, honeymoon, living arrangements, children, and more. It can be difficult to know whether these feelings are a reasonable level of jitters or serious warnings that should be acted on. It's best to pay attention to intuitive messages and discern what is happening. Getting pre-marriage counseling is a reasonable and healthy way of responding to jumpy feelings. Following is a list of some indications of problems that might not go away when the wedding march begins:

- Feeling you were pushed into making a decision or setting a date before you were ready—usually because of not wanting to disappoint your partner or wanting to meet family expectations.

- Loving this person but honestly not having the time or energy it takes to build a life together. Other considerations seem to be in the way—career, children, or plans you've had for a long time regarding travel, hobbies, or time with friends that you aren't willing to give up.
- Having difficulties in blending your families. In fact, it may be beyond your present ability.
- Discovering dishonesty. Something important wasn't disclosed prior to this time—a former marriage, the birth of a child, or a large credit card debt, for example.
- Finding that you aren't able to move ahead but can't identify specifically why. In this case, you probably need to postpone action until your thinking mind catches up with your intuition.

Signs of Relapse

Relapse is a part of the disease of addiction, and there are signs when a person has entered a relapse pattern. Entering the pattern doesn't mean she is using again but is headed that way. Unless something changes, she will use again. When relapse occurs, it's like any other disease or life-threatening situation; it can be the source of greater love or more than a partner or the relationship can stand. If it happens, you will have to explore options with each other and your sponsor or counselor. New boundaries may have to be negotiated and a new agreement formed.

Stress is a common ingredient in the way most of us live, and it is both a relapse trigger and symptom of its onset. Perhaps the most obvious indication of danger is missing recovery meetings or otherwise abandoning a recovery program. Memory problems, over- or underreacting to life's challenges, poor thinking (stinking thinking), inability to maintain a normal routine, and sleep disturbances are other symptoms of relapse or the onset of a new addiction. Any signs of active addiction need to be dealt with immediately.

Emotional warning signs include the following:

- Anger, frustration, tension
- Shame, guilt, hopelessness
- Depression, despondency, despair
- Anxiousness, compulsiveness, nervousness

POTENTIAL ADDICTION PROBLEMS

The following list contains situations that may contribute to a relapse:

- Sexual problems are often indicators of other difficulties. If the problems are about performance, you might want to consult with a health care professional or counselor. If the problems center around fidelity, seek the advice of your sponsor and look into the appropriate Twelve Step meeting or counseling. Just about anything can be resolved if you both decide to try.
- Big financial changes (loss of income or a sudden inheritance) can put a strain on your relationship and trigger a relapse.
- Too much baggage—such as running into old family-of-origin stuff (either yours or your partner's)—can create impossible barriers. This includes past sexual trauma that re-emerges or surfaces for the first time, creating painful memories. Determine

if you can help one another, or get help, or both.
There is suggested reading on relapse prevention
listed in appendix B.

Pain Is Normal, Suffering Is Optional

Breaking up is painful. You need to take steps to avoid slid-
ing into isolation, depression, or active addiction. Especially
dangerous is our tendency to blow it off and look for our
next "victim." Following are some ideas to avoid slipping
into unhealthy behaviors:

- Go to meetings, keep in close touch with program
  friends, and stay tight with your sponsor.
- Establish a nightly emotional check-in time with
  a friend to help fill the intimacy void you'll be
  experiencing.
- Allow yourself to go through the grieving period.
  You can inventory your relationship in due time,
  but for now, just experience your grief and loss.
- If seeing your partner causes pain, stay away. Don't
  engineer "chance" meetings outside the grocery
  store when you know his shopping routine.
- Avoid trips down memory lane, romancing
  your time together. No playing "our" song or
  other sad music. Change your meeting schedule
  if necessary—but keep going to meetings.
- Set boundaries in your head. Take a strong position,
  refusing to revisit the dynamics of the relationship
  or to mull over the breakup. If you are tempted to
  step over these bounds, have an alternative behavior ready: say a prayer, call a friend, tell yourself
  something nice such as "I love you."

- Avoid "shoulding" on yourself—as in "I should have stayed" or "I should have [insert behavior]." Work a Step, any Step, or read the following paragraph on acceptance found in the fourth edition of your Big Book:

And acceptance is the answer to *all* my problems today. When I am disturbed, it is because I find some person, place, thing, or situation—some fact of my life—unacceptable to me, and I can find no serenity until I accept that person, place, thing, or situation as being exactly the way it is supposed to be at this moment. Nothing, absolutely nothing, happens in God's world by mistake. Until I could accept my alcoholism, I could not stay sober; unless I accept life completely on life's terms, I cannot be happy. I need to concentrate not so much on what needs to be changed in the world as on what needs to be changed in me and in my attitudes. (417)

- Have a letting-go ritual where you cut the cords between you and your former partner. Use real ribbon or string and actually cut them. Release the person with appreciation (even if you don't mean it) and take yourself back with love and appreciation (even if you don't want to). You may want to reclaim space you shared as well.

Leave the Trauma-Drama to Scarlett

You might remember the scene from *Gone with the Wind* where Scarlett O'Hara raises her fist to the heavens and declares, "As God is my witness, I'll never go hungry again!"

This is all right for Scarlett but not so good for you. Your tendency will be to deny your emotional pain or hype it. Let's aim for a middle ground, not making more or less out of the situation. Feel the feelings but leave the drama to Scarlett.

You don't have to swear off relationships forever (with God as your witness) or rush ahead to the next one. This is a time for healing and introspection, leaving the future scenarios until later. As a general guide, it's best to wait a year and a half after a marriage or committed relationship. Keep in mind, however, that healing time will be determined by the length of your relationship, the difficulty of your breakup, and the presence of children.

A helpful bit of program wisdom reminds us that while we make conscious choices, we aren't the final authority on how things turn out. It's our job to stay true to our feelings; the way we experienced a relationship is the way we experienced it. Healing comes through telling the truth not by distorting or avoiding reality. We return to self, but we don't have to be alone. Recovery offers support, giving us a community of people who understand the challenge involved and a place to feel valued and be of service.

SUMMARY POINTS

- There are predictable signs of relationship problems, including signs when relapse has entered your world. You can make decisions about how you respond to these signals.
- Sometimes relationships end organically, with no one at fault. Follow a process of letting go and allow yourself to grieve. Later, glean what you can from the experience.

- When you go through a time of consciously "completing" your relationship (rather than a cut-and-run approach), you leave fewer jagged edges and fewer claw marks.
- Identifying your part in the breakup restores a sense of lost power. Take time out to let your heart and head agree. Feel the feelings and interpret your experience. When you follow the process, you grow and make the necessary changes to do it differently the next time around.

CONCLUSION

Building and maintaining an intimate relationship is one of the most complex and difficult challenges life offers. This is true whether you are a recovering person or not. Regardless of your current stage of commitment (including single and reading this book while you think it over), take time to appreciate your willingness to consider something new. While there are no guarantees, removing the blindfold and looking both ways before crossing the street improves your odds of getting to the other side. Following program principles helps you remove the blindfold, and having a dating plan teaches you to look both ways. In time, happy, joyous, and free will be your experience of daily life as you travel the road to happy destiny.

Epilogue

Not even poets have succeeded in defining love to everyone's satisfaction. We know there are different kinds of love. For example, there is the love we instinctively have toward our family or clan that binds us together for survival and has us in its grip whether or not it is earned by those to whom we are bound. Love is often expressed as affection or friendship. There's also agape, a spiritual love that leads people to be of service to humankind. And there is romantic love, a love that binds two people together. As is demonstrated throughout this book, romantic love begins as an emotion or sensation and becomes a behavior. It evolves through a series of conscious choices and agreements rather than simply "happening."

Assuring the next generation was once considered to be the most important aspect of romantic love and marriage. Today we understand the bonding and nurturing aspects of love as well, the ability to cultivate more love, which helps us live a rich, full life. We now know that the best partnerships are between two well-developed individuals who choose to be together rather than the old way in which people sought completion in another. Today we talk about interdependence in relationships rather than independence or dependence.

Yet, individually and as a culture, we're in relationship trouble. Many families are unable to create a healthy and nurturing environment for their offspring. Destructive relationships breed more destructive relationships, with troubled families modeling poor dynamics down through the genera-tions. But regardless of our upbringing, we instinctively seek relationships. So how do we create one that is loving and supportive?

In an attempt to understand yourself better and to heal your wounds, you can focus on the individuals in a rela-tionship or your own family, as you probably have done in your recovery. But the negative patterns you may have dis-covered reflect a bigger societal pattern where power is used to intimidate, shame, and abuse weaker members.

Twelve Step recovery offers a spiritual pattern for friend-ships, work relations, dating, relating, family life, and com-munity. Power is seen as coming from a higher source, and no one has power over anyone else. Each person's story is considered a valuable resource for all and is important to the whole. Each person is responsible to the God of her un-derstanding. The diverse membership is unified through service work—being present to anyone who needs help heal-ing addiction. This transformed and transforming way of being in community carries the promise of altering both the individual and culture for the better.

Probably no one would be more surprised than the founders of AA—Bill Wilson, Dr. Bob, and the handful of others who were there at the beginning. The words of the Big Book, "We shall be with you in the Fellowship of the Spirit," continue to take on new meaning.

There is a simple but profound Lakota prayer: *Mitakuye Oyasin*, which means "all our relations." It acknowledges the essential unity of creation. *Mitakuye Oyasin* honors the sacredness of our individual paths while realizing we are all going somewhere together. It reminds us of the innate sa-credness of all life—weaving together the needs of all people, animals, plants, and the earth itself. On this path, no one has power over anyone or anything. Life depends on finding agreement.

Appendix A ✳

Homework for Extra Credit

EXERCISE 1
BALANCING YOUR MEDICINE WHEEL

Addiction is a disease of body, mind, and spirit, and recovery means healing the *whole* self. Your committee or cast of characters (discussed in chapter 5) offers a way of learning more about hidden drives that influence your decisions, most of which affect your whole self. The medicine circle, found below, can be a helpful tool for maintaining balance in all aspects of life: physical, emotional, mental, and spiritual.

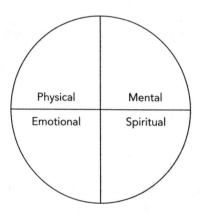

How you divide your time indicates what is important to you. Placing your activities in the various quadrants of the circle lets you see if your life is balanced and which areas to address if it isn't. Following are some ingredients in a well-balanced life. What activities can you add to bring balance? What archetype might help you with those activities?

Physical
- Eat balanced meals at regular intervals
- Get regular checkups with health care professionals
- Maintain regular rest and sleep habits
- Exercise regularly—for example, yoga, tai chi, hiking, swimming, and working out at the gym
- Participate in a sporting activity such as tennis, golf, or basketball

What characters from your committee might help you gain balance in the physical area of your life?

Emotional
- Attend recovery meetings or other support groups
- Maintain regular contact with friends and family
- Be an active member in the community through a social club or group
- Feel, name, and act on emotions appropriately

What characters from your committee might help you gain balance in the emotional area of your life?

Mental/Intellectual
- Read
- Learn a new language
- Complete a degree
- Take a class either for credit or for the heck of it
- Continue to develop your mind—for example, attend lectures or workshops
- Travel
- Watch films

What characters from your committee might help you gain balance in the mental/intellectual area of your life?

Spiritual/Creative

- Join or renew a membership in a church
- Participate in a meditation group
- Read books that will further your spirituality
- Develop your creativity, including areas of interest such as music, art, photography, writing, gardening, and so on
- Visit museums

What characters from your committee might help you gain balance in the spiritual/creative area of your life?

EXERCISE 2
FIVE-POINT QUICK EVALUATION

To help you stay on track and make conscious choices when it comes to dates and dating, this book contains a five-point evaluation form. Each category covers a wide variety of items you'll want to consider about your date before bonding emotionally. Pick the questions that work for you and also add your own. Getting the answers doesn't have to sound like a psychological intake. Once you become familiar with the questions and practice applying them a little, the answers can be gleaned easily in a friendly, twenty-minute conversation.

What you will need: your vision statement, your top three preferences, and absolute deal breakers. Make sure to have these in place before you go on your date. You can mentally or physically fill out the rest of the form when you get home from your date.

My dating intention is _____
_____
_____
_____
_____.

The top three character traits or qualities that I expect in a person I'm dating are

1. _____
2. _____
3. _____

My absolute deal breakers are

1. _____
2. _____
3. _____

When completing the rest of the evaluation, your intention is not to take another's inventory. This exercise is a measure of your ability to be honest and stay true to what you believe is important in a partner. So be humble. This is not an opportunity to knock another down or to laugh at what appear to be shortcomings.

1. Physical Attraction

Chemistry is that somewhat mysterious quality that either attracts you to someone or doesn't. Without it you might as well turn the page because chances are you won't develop a relationship. It takes self-awareness on your part to be able to tell the difference between attraction and addiction. Attraction is admiration. Attraction translates to wanting to get to know somebody—not fantasizing about them. Addiction has that "Hey, baby!" reaction and starts the fantasies rolling. When your addiction begins to do the choosing, the rule is to turn and walk toward the nearest exit—quickly.

The following categories should help you gauge, with a level head, if you have a real attraction to your date.

Health and Fitness

What is his or her level of health and fitness? Consider what qualities are important to you and circle what you discover to be true. Feel free to add more qualities that you feel are important too.

Healthy glow / Dark circles
In shape / Out of shape

Height and weight acceptable / Height and weight not
acceptable

Nonsmoker / Smoker

Comfortable / Nervous

Pleasant smile / Frown or scowl

_____ / _____
_____ / _____
_____ / _____

Posture

One woman bases everything on posture. She avoids "slumpers"
and "strutters" and believes the way a person carries himself tells
all. Consider the person in question and circle one of the following:

Positive posture / Negative posture

Hygiene and Grooming

Drawing from the following list, how does he or she measure up
in general appearance and cleanliness? If you'd like, rate your
date from one to five, with five being the highest.

_____ Body cleanliness (looks clean, smells clean, is clean)
_____ Clothes (look clean, smell clean, are clean)
_____ Teeth clean and breath fresh
_____ Dresses appropriately for the situation
_____ Not reeking of perfume or aftershave
_____ Hair clean and combed

_____ _____
_____ _____
_____ _____

Environment or Surroundings

Cleanliness and order say a lot about a person. How important
these are to you is a matter of personal preference. Consider the
following and, if you wish, add a rating of one to five, as you did
in the previous section.

_____ Is his or her house, apartment, or office clean and orderly?

_____ Is the inside of his or her car reasonably clean?

_____ _____

_____ _____

(One man won't date a woman with a messy car. He says it's a sure sign of deeper trouble!)

2. Communication Skills

A skilled conversationalist searches for common ground; a poor one looks for arguments.

Conversation Style

Circle the best description for each item in the following list:

Makes eye contact / Glances around the room
Tone: Mutual and flowing / Tone: Awkward and one-sided
Listens but offers insights / Too opinionated or no opinion
Pleasant tone of voice / Irritating tone of voice
Natural laugh / Forced laugh

_____ / _____

_____ / _____

Conversation Content

Circle the best description of him or her from the following list:

I am genuinely interested. / I am rolling my eyes and mentally going over my to-do list.
Fresh insights / "Same old same old"
We're being ourselves. / One of us is relying on name-dropping or designer name-dropping (as in "I left my BlackBerry in my Beamer.")
Feels real / Feels pretentious

_____ / _____

_____ / _____

Vocabulary Checklist

Consider the following items. Rate each from one to five if you wish, with five being the highest.

_____ Am I talking down?

_____ Is this person too technical, too far over my head?

_____ Is there way too much hemming and hawing?

_____ Does he or she use foul language to the point where I'm uncomfortable?

_____ _____

_____ _____

3. Common Interests

You'll want to be able to share certain activities or topics with your partner such as bicycling, hiking, music, or travel. Of course you don't have to have everything in common, but you do need to be able to respect differences. One woman turns her thumb down at the first mention of auto racing. She doesn't like it, doesn't want to talk about it, and thinks it's a complete waste of time. That might become a problem. On the other hand, another person might not like racing but may still be able to share vicariously in a partner's excitement.

Put a check mark next to what works for you. Remember, the ability to respect each other's differences is the bottom line.

_____ Hobbies and interests

_____ Employment and economic status

_____ Time considerations (Do we have time for each other?)

_____ Promptness (Is he or she chronically late?)

_____ Culture (Do we enjoy the same type of events?)

_____ General lifestyle

_____ _____

_____ _____

4. Personal Development

The area of personal development may be the most important compatibility factor in establishing a satisfying relationship. It includes values and basic sensitivity—a person's approach to life. Values inform all our choices, even if we're not aware of them. When you chase down all the little disagreements and find out there is a basic difference in values, you will almost always be pulling in opposite directions. Religion or spirituality alone doesn't determine compatibility. You can follow different paths but be headed to the same place.

Place check marks next to the areas where you have concerns:

_____ Life goals
_____ Religious beliefs
_____ Spiritual beliefs
_____ Education level and area of study
_____ Cultural differences
_____ Geographical differences
_____ Political differences
_____ Worldview

_____ _____
_____ _____

5. Marriage or Relationship Status

You need a brief summary of previous significant relationships including marriages, children, and the general condition surrounding his or her relationships today. Following are some questions to consider:

_____ Does this person accept his or her role in any breakups?
_____ How much time has elapsed since the breakups?
_____ Does he or she "bad mouth" former partners?
_____ What is his or her sexual history?
_____ Are there any family-of-origin issues to consider?

_____ _____
_____ _____

EXERCISE 3
INTIMACY SELF-TEST

As you're doing your nightly Tenth Step, notice if an event or in-teraction during the day left you uncomfortable or puzzled. To get to the true source of your discomfort, you need to determine if it was an unresolved emotion from childhood or a challenge in the present that requires your attention. Use the following process to find out which of these scenarios is occurring:

1. Describe in a few paragraphs the event that triggered your feelings.
2. List the emotions you were experiencing and rate the intensity of each using a scale of one to five (unless it was an obvious ten!). Place that number beside the emotion.

   For example:
   _____ Anger
   _____ Shame
   _____ Fear
   _____ Sadness

3. Beginning with the most intense emotion, locate where you feel it in your body.
4. Relax and breathe into it.
5. Is it a familiar feeling?
6. How old do you feel as you feel it?
7. What story goes with this feeling?
8. At the time when the story was happening, what did you need?
9. Can you do that for yourself now?

If you find you are revisiting an unresolved childhood mem-ory, say something nice to yourself. Repeat it as often as possible throughout the day each day and continue deep breathing. The old story eventually heals. If your discomfort is current, identify it and determine if it is something that can be resolved within yourself or with your partner.

EXERCISE 4
BREATHING PRACTICE

Our unexpressed emotional story is stored in the body as chemicals. Each time these feelings are stirred, they restimulate more chemicals, and eventually you become your very own toxic waste site. With a high level of self-awareness, you can observe how you hold your breath when old emotions get stirred up. This is how you hold on to them. Deep breathing is one of the primary ways to eliminate stored toxic emotions from the body. Other ways are through your elimination system (you've heard of being "pissed off").

The best place to begin is simply by taking a few deep breaths and paying attention. Do this at regular intervals throughout the day and you will begin to experience less stress, more clarity, and more energy. The following breathing exercise is a bit of a challenge but worth the effort.

Sit up straight and loosen any tight clothing. Slowly draw your breath in to the count of six. Pay close attention to how the air feels as it enters your nostrils. Feel it going down your windpipe. Expand your belly, and hold the breath for the count of six. Slowly exhale to the count of six. Repeat six times. Later you can add a simple affirmation such as "I draw life (or my Higher Power) into myself, and I exhale my gratitude."

Breathing with a partner is an intimate exercise that creates a spiritual bond. Begin by facing each other and looking into each other's eyes. Slowly begin to breathe together and continue looking at one another. Breath is life. *Inspiration* means the drawing of air into the lungs. It also means to stimulate the human mind to creative thought or to the making of art. Breath also acknowledges divine guidance and influence on human beings; it is a prayer. It is a prayer in which we simply receive the gift of life.

EXERCISE 5
VALUES CLARIFICATION

Values are the strongest indications of compatibility. Chapter 2 included a list of common values many people look for in marriage: love, romance, security, trust, sexual fulfillment, spiritual and psychological growth, happiness, commitment, friendship, communication, shared interests, and a satisfying family life. Other important common values are honesty, compassion, loyalty, creativity, humor, kindness, generosity, and a positive attitude. Values clarification tests can be found at the library or bookstore, or you can make your own according to your likes and dislikes. Identify the attitudes and behaviors you find the most appealing in yourself and those you look for in others and rate them according to their importance to you.

For example, Sam is deeply connected to nature and uses ecological sensitivity to measure potential friendships. He finds that it is a great indicator of values that are important to him: nonmaterialism, global awareness, basic justice and fair play, personal health, and appreciation of and closeness to nature.

Values identify what is at the heart of a person. Behaviors are the outward signs of values; smoking, drinking, using drugs, overeating, stealing, criticizing, stinginess, or overspending tell a lot about a person. Behavior can point out character flaws and also indicate damaged self-esteem. But regardless, you may not want to spend time with someone who is not reflecting a healthy sense of self.

ANSWERS TO SEX QUIZ IN CHAPTER 8

1. b		6. b
2. b		7. b
3. d		8. b
4. a		9. b
5. a		10. b

Appendix B *

Suggested Readings

Alcoholics Anonymous. 4th ed. New York: Alcoholics Anonymous
World Services, 2001.

Atwood, Nina. *Be Your Own Dating Service: A Step-by-Step Guide
to Finding and Maintaining Healthy Relationships.* New York:
Henry Holt and Company, 1996.

Beattie, Melody. *Beyond Codependency: And Getting Better All the
Time.* Center City, Minn.: Hazelden, 1989.

———. *Codependent No More: How to Stop Controlling Others and
Start Caring for Yourself.* Center City, Minn.: Hazelden, 1992.

Bradshaw, John. *Creating Love: The Next Great Stage of Growth.*
New York: Bantam Books, 1994.

———. *Healing the Shame That Binds You.* Deerfield Beach, Fla.:
Health Communications, 1988.

Carnes, Patrick. *Out of the Shadows: Understanding Sexual Addiction.* 3d ed. Center City, Minn.: Hazelden, 2001.

Gorski, Terence T. *Addictive Relationships: Why Love Goes Wrong in
Recovery.* Independence, Mo.: Herald House/Independence
Press, 1993.

———. *Getting Love Right: Learning the Choices of Healthy Intimacy.*
New York: Simon and Schuster, 1993.

Gorski, Terence T., and Merlene Miller. *Staying Sober: A Guide
for Relapse Prevention.* Independence, Mo.: Herald House/
Independence Press, 1986.

Kominars, Sheppard B., and Kathryn D. Kominars. *Accepting
Ourselves and Others: A Journey into Recovery from Addictive and
Compulsive Behaviors for Gays, Lesbians, and Bisexuals.* 2d ed.
Center City, Minn.: Hazelden, 1996.

Norwood, Robin. *Women Who Love Too Much: When You Keep
Wishing and Hoping He'll Change.* New York: J. P. Tarcher, 1985.

Pimental-Habib, Richard. *The Power of a Partner: Creating and Maintaining Healthy Gay and Lesbian Relationships.* Los Angeles: Alyson, 2002.

Schaef, Anne Wilson. *When Society Becomes an Addict.* New York: HarperCollins, 1988.

Schneider, Meg F., and Martine J. Byer. *Sex and the Single Parent: A Guide for Parents Who Find Themselves Back in the Dating Game.* New York: Penguin Putnam, 2002.

Appendix C *

The Twelve Steps of Alcoholics Anonymous

1. We admitted we were powerless over alcohol—that our lives had become unmanageable.
2. Came to believe that a Power greater than ourselves could restore us to sanity.
3. Made a decision to turn our will and our lives over to the care of God *as we understood Him.*
4. Made a searching and fearless moral inventory of ourselves.
5. Admitted to God, to ourselves, and to another human being the exact nature of our wrongs.
6. Were entirely ready to have God remove all these defects of character.
7. Humbly asked Him to remove our shortcomings.
8. Made a list of all persons we had harmed, and became willing to make amends to them all.
9. Made direct amends to such people wherever possible, except when to do so would injure them or others.
10. Continued to take personal inventory and when we were wrong promptly admitted it.
11. Sought through prayer and meditation to improve our conscious contact with God *as we understood Him,* praying only for knowledge of His will for us and the power to carry that out.
12. Having had a spiritual awakening as the result of these steps, we tried to carry this message to alcoholics, and to practice these principles in all our affairs.

The Twelve Steps of AA are from *Alcoholics Anonymous*, 4th ed., published by AA World Services, Inc., New York, N.Y., 59–60.

Index

abandonment, 43–44
ACA (Adult Children of
    Alcoholics), 23–24
acceptance, 3–4, 33–34, 185, 191
    of the past, 42–43, 47
acquaintance rape. *See* date
    rape
addiction, 197, 200
    as "bio-psycho-social"
        disease, 7
    boundaries and, 54, 60
    emotional development
        and, 10, 72, 146
    family history and, 7–9, 11
    relationships and, 7–13
    sexual, 136–37, 139–40
Addictive Relationships (Gorski),
    119–20
Adult Children of Alcoholics
    (ACA), 23–24
agape, 195
Alcoholics Anonymous, 167,
    196, 211
anal sex, 149
anger, 9, 180
apologizing, 110, 185–86
archetypes, 71–72, 197
    dating and, 80–83
    as dream team, 80
    the fool, 79, 80, 85
    higher self, 79, 85

the lover, 79, 80–82, 84
purpose of, 72, 73, 83, 85
the rebel, 74, 76–77, 78, 80, 85
the toxic adult, 78, 80
the toxic parent, 74–75, 78,
    80, 129, 184
the warrior, 79, 80, 81–82, 84
the wounded child, 75, 77,
    78, 80, 84, 85, 129, 184
arguments, 128–30
attraction, 24, 25, 26, 151,
    200–202
avoidance, 9

Beattie, Melody, 11
Big Book, 47, 116, 191, 196
bisexuals, 167–68, 169–70
blaming, 183
body language, 55, 99–100
boundaries
    abusive experiences and,
        61–62
    addiction and, 54, 60
    archetypal warrior and, 81
    body talk and, 55
    breaking up and, 190
    dating and, 23, 68, 110
    emotional, 58–59
    external, 53, 55
    internal, 53, 56
    mental, 59

as natural defenses, 53–54, 55
negotiable, 54, 57, 69
non-negotiable, 54–55,
    67–68
physical, 58, 61–62, 141
purpose of, 53, 54
during relationship time-
    outs, 181
spiritual, 59–60
brain functions, 121–22, 124, 136
pleasure centers as, 142–43
breaking up, 23–24, 30–31, 36,
    67–68
acting-out behaviors prior
    to, 179–80
avoiding unhealthy behav-
    ior following, 190–92
childhood issues in, 186–87
communications during, 185
conscious process of, 183–86
due to intimacy/commit-
    ment issues, 178–79
healing time needed after,
    192
identifying patterns in, 178
let's-be-friends trap in, 185
marriages, 180–81
reasons to resist, 180
thinking/feeling dilemma
    in, 177–78
breathing exercises, 206–7

ceremonies, 45–47, 191
children, 34
in addictive families, 8–9,
    10, 11, 33, 75
coping behaviors of, 42–43

of dating couples, 163–67
early nurturing of, 142–43
inner vision of, 47
violence experienced by,
    50–51
choices, conscious, 3
to break up, 183–86
in dating, 12, 17, 23, 36–37
through dating plan, 24
in partner selection, 25
regarding sexual intimacy,
    135, 137, 139, 141
to remain single, 35
codependency, 11–13, 171
Co-dependents Anonymous
    (CoDA), 23–24
commitment
exclusivity and, 154–55, 171
to recovery, 4, 5, 22, 29,
    110–11
to a relationship, 28–30, 128,
    155–56, 178–79
to self, 21, 25, 27, 29, 30
sexual relationships and,
    139–40, 145–46
communication
during arguments, 128–29
during a breakup, 185
concerning sexual activity,
    28–29, 145, 146
HALT and, 130
skills needed for, 97–99,
    126–28, 202–3
compatibility, 130–33, 178–79,
    203–4, 207
compliments, 97
condoms, 147–48, 149

control, 33, 74–75, 77, 78
corpus callosum, 121
counseling, 187–88
counter-dependency, 11, 12
courage, 34
creativity, 75

date rape, 62–63, 65–67
   drugs used in, 65–66
   myths about, 63
dating
   analyzing feelings/out-
      comes of, 104–5, 110,
      152–53
   archetypes and, 80–83
   children and, 163–67
   conscious choices about, 12,
      17, 23, 36–37
   conversation tips for, 97–99
   designing plan for. *See* dat-
      ing plan
   disclosing past experiences
      in, 153, 204
   evaluating partner during,
      116–18, 197, 199–205
   in gay community, 102,
      168–72
   getting started, 94, 95–96,
      109–10, 151–53, 165
   ideal time to begin, 5–6, 10,
      151
   initiating, 102–4
   lifestyle differences and,
      132–33, 197–99
   online, 90–91
   paying for, 108–9
   places to avoid, 89–91, 106–7

places to go, 105–6, 107
   as process, 3, 4, 5, 35, 90,
      113, 139
   as recovering couple, 89–90,
      159–63
   selecting a partner during,
      24–26, 119, 133
   for seniors, 172–74
   spiritual principles applied
      to, 31–32
   "sport," 4–5
   things to do, 105–6
   transportation for, 107–8
   traps to avoid, 13–15, 62–69,
      96–97, 103, 136
   unhealthy past relation-
      ships and, 39
dating plan, 24
   designing, 113–14
   following, 136
   Higher Power in, 49, 116, 154
   list making in, 113–14, 116–18
denial, 8–9
destiny, 47
disagreements, 128–30
dopamine, 136
Dr. Bob, 167, 196
drugs, date-rape, 65–66
dysfunctional families, 7–9, 11,
   195–96

Easy Does It Dating Game,
   150–56
Ecstasy, 66
emotional bonding, 4, 26, 27,
   119, 153–54
emotional compatibility, 131

emotional development, 10, 72,
146
inner voices and. *See*
archetypes
emotional intimacy, 118,
119–20, 126, 130
emotional quotient (EQ), 131
emotional well-being, 198
emotions, 56–57, 60–61
See also brain functions
boundaries and, 58–59
ending a relationship and,
177, 183–84, 185, 191–92
expressing, 123, 128–30
as human impulses, 120, 121
identifying/interpreting,
120, 122–23, 205–6
indicating relapse, 189
intimacy as, 118, 119–20,
126
love as, 141
pair bonding and, 136,
153–54
provide information, 120–22
repressed, 123
triggers for, 123–24, 126–27
unexpressed, 122–24, 206
engagements, 29
exclusivity, 154–55, 171

families
addictive, 8–9, 10, 11, 33, 75
dysfunctional, 7–9, 11,
195–96
fear
of abandonment, 43–44
of change, 179–80
letting go of, 49

of losing control, 33
of rejection, 95
flirting, 100–102
forgiveness, 34
Fourth Step
ceremony with, 46
on past romantic relationships, 39–45
reveals hidden assump-
tions, 40

gay men, 167–72
dating standards and, 102
role models for, 171
social circles of, 169–71
Twelve Step meetings and,
168–69
Getting Love Right (Gorski),
139
GHB, 65
God. *See* Higher Power
Gone with the Wind, 191–92
Gorski, Terence, 23, 119–20, 139
gratitude, 115
grieving, 19–20, 171
a lost relationship, 30, 31,
185, 190
guilt, 30, 164–65, 171

HALT, 130
Healthy Relationship Pyramid,
150
Higher Power, 80
ceremonies and, 46
conscious contact with,
31–32, 48
in dating plan, 49, 116, 154
expressing gratitude to, 115

HIV/AIDS, 146, 149, 171
homophobia, 168, 169–70
homosexuals. *See* bisexuals; gay
     men; lesbians
honesty, 95, 113, 164
     in analyzing self, 114–15
     concerning potential part-
          ner, 116–18, 197
     concerning sexual orienta-
          tion, 168
HOW (honest, open, willing),
     113

intellectual compatibility, 130
intellectual well-being, 198
Internet dating services, 90–91
intimacy, 118–20, 193
     with another, 6, 27, 29, 125,
          128, 178–79
     avoidance and, 9
     definition of, 119–20
     emotions and, 118, 119–20,
          126
     as healthy desire, 2, 4, 17
     listening and, 125
     phases of, 118, 150
     with self, 21, 22, 30, 125
     self-revelation and, 118
     sexual relationships and,
          145–46, 155

judging, 127, 141

ketamine, 65–66

lesbians
     codependency and, 171
     social circles of, 169–70

support systems for, 171
     Twelve Step meetings and,
          168, 169
letting go, 49, 116, 191
lifestyles, 132–32, 197–99
listening, 98–99, 125, 127–28,
     177–78
love, 141, 195
     of self, 143, 144
lying, 102

marriage
     breaking up, 180–81
     counseling prior to, 187–88
     expectations for, 18
     serial monogamy as, 19
masturbation, 145
medicine wheel, 197–99
men
     flirting behavior of, 101–2
     sexual behavior of, 63–64
Mitakuye Oyasin, 196

Niebuhr, Reinhold, 32
norepinephrine, 136

online dating, 90–91
oral sex, 149
oxytocin, 142

pair bonding, 136, 153–54, 177
parents, single, 163–67
parents, toxic, 74–75, 78
partner selection, 24–26
     factors affecting, 137–38
     moving slowly with, 24, 25
phenylethylamine (PEA), 136
pheromones, 137

physical attraction, 200–202
physical compatibility, 131
physical well-being, 58, 61–62,
    141, 198
pleasure centers, 142–43
powerlessness, 184
prayer, 116, 196, 207
    See also Serenity Prayer
prenuptial counseling, 187–88
problem solving, 125, 128–30,
    178, 180–83
promiscuity, 140–41
purification, 46

rape. See date rape
rape crisis centers, 63, 68
rapport building, 99–100
rebelliousness, 74
recovering couples, 89–90,
    159–63
    advantages of dating for,
        159–60
    disadvantages of dating for,
        160
    meeting schedules of, 160–61
    relapses of, 161–62
    values of, 159–60
recovery, 17, 159, 178
    See also archetypes; recover-
        ing couples; relapses
    commitment to, 4, 5, 22, 29,
        110–11
    control issues during, 116
    emotional development
        and, 10, 146
    finding wisdom in, 34–35
    grieving and, 19–20

process of, 34, 53–54, 77, 197
relationships and. See
    relationships
same-sex meetings during,
    168
seniors in, 172
sexual relationships and, 137
as time of nurturing, 143–44
as time of self-discovery, 21
time required for, 13
rejection, 30, 95
relapses, 137, 188–90
    patterns leading to, 4–5,
        188–90
    recovering couples and,
        161–62
    triggers for, 188–89
relationships
    See also boundaries; dating;
        intimacy
    with abusive persons, 61, 196
    beginning stages of, 26–28
    commitment to, 28–30, 128,
        155–56
    compatibility in, 130–33,
        203–4
    complicated by addiction,
        7–13
    cycling of, 19
    emotional triggers in,
        123–24, 126–27
    ending. See breaking up
    hanging on to, 36, 180
    healthy, 1–3, 150–56
    ideal picture of, 18, 29–30,
        137–38
    as mirrors, 116

myths about, 35–37
pair bonding in, 136,
    153–54, 177
problem solving in, 125,
    128–30, 178, 181–83
reasons for failure of, 139
of recovering couples. *See*
    recovering couples
with self, 4, 5
serial monogamy in, 19
sexual. *See* sexual
    relationships
sexual abuse survivors and,
    61–62, 189
sharing program wisdom
    in, 162–63
skills needed for, 3, 5–6, 8,
    21, 23, 26, 27, 29
taking time-outs from, 181
thinking/feeling aspects of,
    120, 122–23, 124, 187–88
through expanded social
    circles, 92–95, 169–70
trust in, 125
resentment, 180
restaurant tips, 107
rituals, 45–47, 191
Rohypnol, 65
romanticizing, 9–10, 37

same-sex dating. *See* gay men;
    lesbians
self-awareness, 4, 5, 17, 123, 206
    role of archetypes in, 72–73,
    87
self-care, 144
self-defeating patterns, 39–40, 41

self-determination, 17
self-discovery, 20–22, 31, 91–92
self-esteem, 11, 12, 116
self-knowledge, 125
self-worth, 45
seniors, dating, 172–74
sensuousness, 142–45
serenity, 32–33, 137, 144–45
Serenity Prayer, 32–35
Sex and Love Addicts
    Anonymous (SLAA), 45
sexual abuse survivors, 61–62,
    189
sexual activity
    addictive, 136–37, 139–40
    confused with love, 141
    as lust and chemicals,
        136–37
    making choices about, 141
    as power, 63
    safe, 140, 142, 147–49
sexual innuendos, 67, 101
sexually transmitted diseases
    (STDs), 146, 148–49
sexual relationships
    choices concerning, 135,
        137, 139
    commitment and, 139–40,
        145–46
    communication in, 28–29,
        145, 146
    for couples with children,
        165–66
    dramatic changes in, 138–39
    gender and, 63–64
    intimacy and. *See* intimacy
    physical compatibility in, 131

recovery and, 137
relapse and, 189
sensuousness and, 142, 143
spirituality and, 142
vulnerability in, 142
single, being
conscious choice of, 35
parenting and, 163–67
recurrence of, 19
as time of self-discovery,
20–22
sobriety, 167–68
socializing, 92–94, 169–70
South Eastern Centre Against
Sexual Assault, 63
spiritual compatibility, 131–32
spirituality, 130
dating and, 31–32
problem solving and,
180–81
sexual experiences and, 142
trauma and, 45
Twelve Step programs and,
130, 196
spiritual well-being, 56–60, 196,
199
stalking, 68
STDs (sexually transmitted
diseases), 146, 148–49
stress, 188
surrender, 116

Tenth Step, 36, 185, 205
Third Step, 116
Third Tradition, 167–68
time-outs, 181

transcendence, 142
trauma, 45
trust, 125, 142
Twelve Step meetings, 190, 192
finding dates at, 89–90
gay communities and,
167–68, 169
Twelve Step programs, 95, 167
principles of, 3, 211
spirituality and, 130, 196

uniqueness, 10–11
unworthiness, 43, 45

values, 24, 131–32, 159–60, 204,
207
vibrators, 145
violence, 9, 50–51, 136
visions, 47–48, 49
vision statement, 48–50, 115
vulnerability, 26–27, 89–90,
100
in sexual experiences, 142
of women, 103

willingness. See compatibility
Wilson, Bill, 167, 196
wisdom, 34–35, 172–73
wish list, 116–18
women
flirting behavior of, 101
initiating dates, 102
new options for, 18
sexual behavior of, 63–64
vulnerability of, 103
workplace romances, 91

About the Author

Mary Faulkner has been a lifelong student of spirituality and holds a master's degree in religious education. She was the executive editor and a staff writer for *Recovering Magazine* in San Francisco and has published several books on the topics of religion, spirituality, and recovery, including *The Complete Idiot's Guide to Understanding Catholicism* and *The Complete Idiot's Guide to Women's Spirituality*. In addition to having a counseling practice, Faulkner teaches, holds workshops, and travels. She has three grown children and three grandchildren.